What Every Christian Needs to Know

Register This New Book

Benefits of Registering*

- ✓ FREE **replacements** of lost or damaged books
- ✓ FREE **audiobook** – *Pilgrim's Progress,* audiobook edition
- ✓ FREE information about new titles and other **freebies**

www.anekopress.com/new-book-registration

*See our website for requirements and limitations.

What Every Christian Needs to Know

Saved to Serve

Steps to a Wonderful Life of Winning Souls for Christ

HOWARD W. POPE

Bible Teacher and Evangelist at
The Moody Bible Institute of Chicago

We enjoy hearing from our readers. Please contact
us at www.anekopress.com/questions-comments
with any questions, comments, or suggestions.

Cover Designer: J. Martin

Editor: Larry Oats

Aneko Press

www.anekopress.com

Aneko Press, Life Sentence Publishing, and our logos are trademarks of

Life Sentence Publishing, Inc.
203 E. Birch Street
P.O. Box 652
Abbotsford, WI 54405

RELIGION / Christian Living / Spiritual Growth

Paperback ISBN: 979-8-88936-236-4
eBook ISBN: 979-8-88936-237-1
10 9 8 7 6 5 4 3 2
Available where books are sold

Contents

Preface

According to Isaiah 53:6, one needs to know two things and do one thing to become a Christian.

Having become a Christian, he needs to realize that with the gospel in hand, he has more to give to this world than the whole world has to give to him.

If he will study human nature and how to approach it, if he will study the Bible and how to apply it, and, above all, if he will hold up Christ with the absolute assurance that the Spirit will bless his effort every time he does it, he cannot fail to succeed. "My word will not return to Me empty."

This book is designed to help those who wish to engage in personal evangelism and whose experience is so limited that they will welcome suggestions from another.

Howard W. Pope

Chapter 1

First, Be Sure You Yourself Are Truly Saved

his topic may seem superfluous to some, but it is not.
Many Christians have no real assurance of salvation.
They have a hope, but it is not a sure hope. They do not have
a clear idea of what the Christian life is and had no evident
emotional experience when they entered it. Therefore, they
are constantly harassed by doubts as to whether or not they
are Christians. As long as they are in this condition, they can
hardly lead others to Christ. This is undoubtedly one reason
so many are reluctant to engage in personal evangelism; they
are unsure of their own salvation.

Some think it presumptuous for someone to say he knows
he is a Christian. Paul evidently does not agree with them, for
he says, *I know whom I have believed and I am convinced that
He is able to guard what I have entrusted to Him until that day*

(2 Timothy 1:12b). From 1 John 5:13, we learn that God intends that all His children shall know whose children they are. *These things I have written to you who believe in the name of the Son of God, so that you may know that you have eternal life.* 1 John 3:1 teaches the same doctrine of assurance: *See how great a love the Father has bestowed on us, that we would be called children of God; and such we are. For this reason the world does not know us, because it did not know Him.*

It is not important that one knows *when* he became a Christian, but it is very important that he knows that he *is* a Christian. Those converted in childhood often have no recollection of when they were converted, and it is not necessary that they should. It is necessary, however, that they should know that they are converted if they are to have any joy or efficiency in Christian work. We come then to a question vital to multitudes of troubled souls in all our churches: "Can one know that he is a Christian, and what are the grounds of such assurance?" There are three unmistakable proofs of the believer's salvation.

1. The witness of God's Word. The forgiveness of sin takes place in the mind of God, not in the emotional nature of the believer. Our first and best evidence of any such transaction must be the testimony of God Himself. If I comply with the conditions established by God for the forgiveness of sin, I know that my sins are forgiven because I have God's word for it. If I accept Jesus Christ as my personal Savior, I know I have become a child of God because God's Word affirms it. It is not a question of how I feel but what God says. The feeling may be wholly lacking, yet the transaction may be nonetheless real.

Suppose a couple stands up to be married. The minister asks, "Do you take this woman to be your wife?" "I do." "Do you take this man to be your husband?" "I do." He then pronounces them husband and wife. As the couple turns around to receive congratulations, suppose you ask them if they feel they are married. The chances are that they will reply, "No, we cannot say that we do." However, they are married, whether they realize it or not. Those simple words spoken in the presence of witnesses make them husband and wife. It is not a question of feeling but simply one of fact. However, if they faithfully perform the duties of their new relationship, all the joys of married life will come to them in due time.

The yielding of the heart to Christ and the coming of the Spirit may occur without any emotional consciousness and yet be just as real as if accompanied by floods of feeling. However, if believers faithfully perform the duties of their new relationship, all the joys of the Christian life will soon be theirs. *He who has My commandments and keeps them . . . I will disclose Myself to him* (John 14:21). We have been so accustomed to the idea that the conviction of sin is the only door through which one can enter the Christian life, that many good Christians who accepted Christ without any such conviction question the reality of their conversion. There is a conviction of righteousness as well as a conviction of sin. Conviction of righteousness is often the impelling motive that leads children raised in Christian homes to accept Christ. However, the motive matters little so long as it leads to a vital union with the Son of God.

> *There is a conviction of righteousness as well as a conviction of sin.*

Dr. A. J. Gordon once dealt with a lady who claimed to have accepted Christ but did not feel saved. All efforts to help her were unsuccessful until he finally asked if she owned the house where she lived. She said she did. "Do you have a certain 'at home' feeling in this house which you do not have in any other?" "Yes." "Is that why you know the house is yours?" "Certainly not. I suppose I might feel as much at home in a house that was not mine if I lived in it long enough." "How, then, do you know this house is yours?" "Because I have the deed which conveys the property to me and have read it with my own eyes." "You are sure this house is yours because the record says so?" "Yes." "And you would be just as sure even if you did not have that peculiar 'at home' feeling of which you speak?" "I think so. The feeling is delightful, but it is no proof of ownership."

"Now, if you could see a deed by which God had given you eternal life, would you believe the record?" "I certainly would." "Would that record be sufficient to convince you without additional evidence?" "I think it would." He then asked her to read 1 John 5:11-12, *And the testimony is this, that God has given us eternal life, and this life is in His Son. He who has the Son has the life; he who does not have the Son of God does not have the life.* When she read the verses, he asked her if she knew she was saved. She said, "I do." "How do you know it?" "Because I have God's word for it."

2. The witness of the Spirit. *The Spirit Himself testifies with our spirit that we are children of God* (Romans 8:16). The witness of God's Word is sufficient to prove that one is a child of God. If one does not believe this witness, he makes God a liar (1 John 5:10). However, the believer is also entitled to the witness of the Spirit and should not be satisfied until he has it. It is part of his inheritance in Christ Jesus; if he has not received it, he should reverently but persistently inquire why.

> The believer is entitled to the witness of the Spirit and should not be satisfied until he has it.

In some cases where the witness of the Spirit is lacking, the person has likely made no confession of Christ. Matthew 10:32 shows that when we confess Christ before others, He confesses us before the Father. Romans 10:9 and 1 John 5:10 indicate that when we confess to the world that we have Jesus as our Savior, the Spirit witnesses in our hearts that we are saved. At once, we have different feelings towards God. Before we called Him God, the Supreme Being, or the Deity, but now we think of Him and call Him Father. The reason for this is evident. We have been born of the Spirit and become His children, and now He is our Father. *Because you are sons, God has sent forth the Spirit of His Son into our hearts, crying, 'Abba! Father!'* (Gal. 4:6).

A friend of mine was accosted by a lady at the close of a service. She told him that she had been trying to lead a Christian life for years but had never enjoyed any assurance. She was a woman of intelligence and refinement. He questioned her carefully, and she answered all his questions with the utmost frankness and candor. She knew of nothing in her life that was displeasing to God. Finally, he asked if she had ever confessed Christ. To his surprise, she answered in the negative. She was waiting until she had the inward assurance that she was saved before making an outward confession of her faith. He showed her from the Bible that she was reversing God's order, which is first confession and then the witness of the Spirit. The next night, she was in the meeting. When an opportunity occurred, she arose and quietly said, "Friends, I wish to make a public confession of my faith in Jesus Christ."

The next day, my friend met someone on the street who inquired if he had heard about Mrs. _____. "No, what about her?" "Why, last night she went to her neighbor's house after they had retired and rang the bell. They opened the window and inquired who was there. She answered, 'It is Mrs._____. I have confessed Christ as my Savior tonight and am so happy that I cannot contain myself. All my life, I have been robbing Him of my influence and myself of His joy. O friends, do confess Christ as your Savior!'" She went from house to house for half the night, ringing doorbells, telling of her joy, and urging people to confess Christ.

3. The fruit of the Spirit. *But the fruit of the Spirit is love, joy, peace, patience, kindness, goodness, faithfulness* (Gal. 5:22). This is the evidence our neighbors will appreciate most and which ought to be apparent to all. It does not appear all at once, however, for fruit grows, and growth requires time, while a gift is bestowed instantly.

Chapter 2

You Are Saved to Serve

In his letter to the church in Rome, Paul says, *I am under obligation both to Greeks and to barbarians, both to the wise and to the foolish* (Romans 1:14). When and where did Paul discover that he was "obligated," in debt to the very edge of bankruptcy? Not in the theological school in Jerusalem. More likely, it was on the way to Damascus. God drew aside the veil which hides the earthly from the heavenly and gave him a glimpse of the risen and glorified Jesus. He learned more theology in that one moment than in all the years he had spent at the feet of Gamaliel. That little revelation of Jesus wrought a revolution in Saul. That is what revelations are for. As soon as he became acquainted with Jesus, he believed everyone else ought to know Him. That priceless knowledge was a sacred trust, and he was a debtor to everyone who did not know Him.

Something of the same kind occurs at every true conversion.

We realize that our relationship with this world has changed almost as much as our relationship with God. This is a lost world, and while we are still in it, we are no longer of it. We belong to the life-saving service, and it is our business to help seek and save the lost. As we go through life, we no longer ask, "How much can we get out of this world? But rather, how much can we put into it?" With Jesus Christ to draw upon, every one of us has more to give to the world than the whole wide world has to give to us. "I'm a child of the King, I'm a child of the King." The threefold obligation to serve our day and generation arises from the following:

1. From the commands of the Lord Jesus. No one can read the New Testament without noticing that He expects every one of His followers to become a soul-winner. He taught the world for thirty years by example and three years by precept. Then, at the close of His earthly career, He uttered one command, "Go into all the world and preach the Gospel to every creature." That command remains in force to this day. *You did not choose Me*, He says, *but I chose you, and appointed you that you would go and bear fruit, and that your fruit would remain, so that whatever you ask of the Father in My name He may give to you* (John 15:16). Here then is the Christian's call and commission to be a personal worker. Couple these commands with such ringing utterances as *You are My friends if you do what I command you* (John 15:14) and *Why do you call Me, "Lord, Lord," and do not do what I say?* (Luke 6:46). We must either quit calling Jesus "Lord," or we must go about the Master's business.

2. From the nature of the gospel itself. It is "good news," and therefore, it must be carried to the individual by an individual. We hear much about reaching the masses and regenerating society, but we must not forget that society is composed of individuals. Sin is an individual matter, and

so is salvation. The world will not be judged by nations or townships, but *each one of us will give an account of himself to God* (Romans 14:12). Jesus taught the crowds, but when He forgave people's sins, He did it one by one. *You will be gathered up one by one, O sons of Israel* (Isaiah 27:12). The gospel is so simple that even a child can understand it. However, sin is so subtle, and the needs of men are so varied that it often requires an experienced worker to apply the gospel to the individual successfully.

> *Sin is an individual matter, and so is salvation.*

One sinner thinks he is not very bad, and another is afraid he cannot hold out. Still others have doctrinal difficulties of various kinds. What is worse still is that most of them are not quite ready to do their duty when they see it without some persuasion. Hence, no amount of preaching can ever replace the personal worker.

3. The changed religious conditions require it. In the past, it was customary for people to attend church. Indeed, one was hardly counted respectable unless he did. That day has gone by. The world no longer comes to the church for the gospel. The majority of the people today do not attend church. One reason for this is the strenuous life that many lead. They work so hard through the week that they consume seven days' strength in six days. When Sunday comes, they are so exhausted that they think they cannot attend church. Many working men receive such small wages that they cannot provide suitable clothing. Even if they do go, the contrast between their humble home and the elegant church is often so striking as to be painful. In many churches, the gospel has been replaced with a cheap substitute. "The ministers preach over our heads" is a common complaint among poor people. Occasionally,

though not usually, a church is so cold and formal that a stranger is not likely to enter a second time.

The story is told about a poor man once applied for admission to a wealthy church. The committee saw that he would add nothing to their financial strength or social standing and recommended that he wait a while. To their surprise, he soon appeared again. At a loss of words, one of them suggested that he talk with the Lord about the matter. The man meekly consented and went away. In a few weeks, he appeared before the committee again. They were now at their wits' end, but determined to contest every step of the way, they inquired, "Brother, did you talk with the Lord about this matter?" "I did." "And what did He say?" "He told me not to get discouraged, but to be as patient as I could. He said He had been trying to get into this church Himself ever since it was organized, but that He had not yet succeeded." This story may seem a little exaggerated, but it is to be feared that there are not a few churches where such an interview might occur.

For these and other reasons, a large part of every community practically ignores the church. When this is the case, there is only one alternative: the church must carry the gospel to the world, for the gospel they must have. But who is to do it? The laymen and women. They know the people; they meet them in shops, stores, and on the street. They know their needs and disposition as a minister cannot. This is the New Testament idea: "To every man his work." The church is not a field upon which the minister is to spend his strength but a force which he is to organize and lead in the conquest of the world. The church will never achieve any marked success until she trains and puts every available man, woman, and child to work.

Chapter 3

We Have a Message Worth Proclaiming

The world has always been willing to listen to a man with a real message from heaven. Since the days of John the Baptist, whenever anyone has manifestly been sent from God and has borne witness of the Truth, the people have turned out to hear him. Luther in his day and Wesley and Whitefield in theirs were recognized as true messengers of God. Fifty years ago, George Williams spoke one of God's thoughts, and today 5,000 Young Men's Christian Associations affirm the value of his utterance.

William Carey brought another great thought from heaven, and Robert Raikes another. In our own land, Dwight L. Moody, Francis E. Clark, Anthony Comstock, and Frances Willard have been bearers of rich messages from God. All these have met with stout opposition, for *My thoughts are not your thoughts*. Eventually, their message was received and incorporated into the life of the church.

"One accent of the Holy Ghost,
The heedless world hath never lost."

No one can doubt that God has messages for the church of today. Never was there an age that needed divine wisdom more than ours. Great problems confront us, and great dangers threaten us. Many of God's people seem dazed by the difficulties before them and cry out in pitiful tones, "Who is sufficient for these things?" Instead of waiting upon God for a renewal of their strength, they resort to worldly expedients to gain the attention of the fickle crowd. Others recognize the same difficulties and dangers and clamor loudly for "A man with a message." They seem to be looking for a great spiritual leader who towers above his fellows like Elijah or John the Baptist and who, by the excellence of his vision and the moral grandeur of his life, commands attention and inspires confidence.

It may be that God will raise up another Elijah. Indeed, more than one has already been declared to be the prophet of the twentieth century. It is certainly easier to wait and wish for some great man to be raised up than to listen ourselves to the Word of God, but who shall say that the latter way is not more in accordance with the divine plan?

Every Christian should be "A man with a message." Was it not said of our day, *I will pour out My Spirit on all mankind; And your sons and daughters will prophesy, Your old men will dream dreams, Your young men will see visions* (Joel 2:28). Was it not said of all believers, *You shall be My witnesses* (Acts 1:8)?

Surely God needs us all as messengers of mercy to this sin-stricken world. Yet, how many seem to have no message? They have nothing to say for God because they have heard nothing, and they hear nothing because they are not living in communion with Him. They are like a broken telephone, which can neither receive nor transmit. Their call is dropped, their communication broken, and they are of no use.

How important it is then that those who are in open communication with God should take time to be holy, receive the messages of God, and deliver them to the world.

How to Obtain a Message

There are grave obstacles in the paths of even those who are busiest in the service of God. This is an age of hurry and worry. Unless we are very careful, we shall fall into the spirit of the age and allow ourselves to be robbed of that quiet and rest essential to a deep acquaintance with God. Somehow, we must take time to be alone with God and let the truth about Jesus saturate our whole lives with its spirit. So shall

We must take time to be alone with God and let the truth about Jesus saturate our whole lives.

we leave our prayer time each day with the dew of heaven upon our hearts and a fresh message upon our lips. *He who has an ear, let him hear what the Spirit says to the churches* (Rev. 2:29).

One great mistake made by the church in the past was to suppose that the minister was the only man with a message from God. That left the church largely dependent upon the Christian experience of one individual. If he did not get the message from God, the congregation suffered. If the Word of God was not radiant in his eyes and the music of heaven did not vibrate in his heart, their souls would grow lean, and their strength diminished. Now the teaching is different. "To every man his work," and "To every man some manifestation of the Spirit."

It is almost pathetic as one reads the Scriptures to see how eager God is to share His great thoughts with His children and how reluctant they are to receive them. *An ox knows its owner, And a donkey its master's manger, But Israel does not know, My people do not understand* (Isaiah 1:3). *Oh that My people would listen to Me, that Israel would walk in My ways! I would quickly subdue their enemies and turn My hand against their adversaries* (Psalm 81:13-14). *I said, "Here am I, here am I" . . . to a nation which did not call on My name. I have spread out My hands all day long to a rebellious people* (Isaiah 65:2). *I have many more things to say to you, but you cannot bear them now* (John 16:12). *Things which eye has not seen and ear has not heard, and which have not entered the heart of man, all that God has prepared for those who love Him* (1 Cor. 2:9).

It is a dangerous thing to know God's will and not do it. One of the most perilous things a Christian can do is simply to hold his own and not go forward into the deep things of God when led by the Spirit. I have read of a Christian man who became so engrossed in his business that he essentially lost his fellowship with God. After a while, his business began to fail; he found that in a few weeks, the vein of coal from which he had been mining would be exhausted, and all his investment would be useless. He was also impressed that his business troubles were due to his departure from God, which led him to much prayer.

One night, in a dream, a voice seemed to say to him, "Go deeper." It seemed to him to be the voice of God, and it led to an entire transformation of his life. As he entered upon a closer walk with God, his heart was filled with new joy and power. Still, the voice kept speaking to him so persistently that he began to think it had something to do with his business. So one day, he proposed to his foreman that they should abandon the old vein of coal and sink a new shaft to find a deeper vein. The foreman ridiculed the idea, for all the indications were against it. He insisted, and a shaft was sunk. After they had gone down a reasonable distance, they struck not a vein of coal but an immense vein of iron. Suddenly, the bankrupt miner found himself a millionaire. He had gone deeper and found iron instead of coal. At the same time, he had sunk a spiritual shaft into the deep things of God and was now reveling in the true riches of the Holy Ghost.

Is not this God's message to us today? "Go deeper." If we have exhausted all the satisfaction and power in our present knowledge of truth, let us enter into the deep things of God, the depths of wisdom, love, peace, and power. God yearns to impart to us His very best, and He will do it just as soon as we are ready to receive it.

Do Not Belittle the Message

While the responsibility of receiving and transmitting God's thoughts is distributed to the whole church, the danger is that many will think that their message is of little value. "If I could speak and pray like such a one, it would be worthwhile," they say. A messenger boy might also say, "This telegram is a short one and doubtless of little importance, and so I will not hurry about delivering it." What does he know about its value? Nothing at all. It may be the most important message received at the office for a year. Even so, our testimony, short and stammering though it be, may, in God's sight, be the most important message of the meeting. Let us never withhold it when God bids us speak. Let us never dishonor the *Let us never withhold when God bids us speak.* Holy Spirit by thinking that what He prompts us to say is of little consequence because our gifts are not as showy as some. God loves diversity. Remembering that a small copper wire, if clean and well insulated, is a better conductor than the largest gold or silver wire, let us not envy the gifts of others but keep our own in constant use and give to the world all the precious thoughts that God has revealed to us.

"Dwell deep, O my soul, deeper yet, hour by hour.
Dwell deep, deeper yet, in His fullness of power."

Chapter 4

Spiritual Gifts and How to Find Them

In the twelfth chapter of First Corinthians, and often in Paul's writings, the church is represented as the body of which Christ is the head. As the head directs the body and through it gives expression to its will, so Christ expresses His will through the church, which is His body.

Every believer is united to and becomes a member of the body of Christ at conversion. Each member has some function to perform, just as the hand or eye has in the physical body. "To every man his work."

Since each member has some function to perform, he also has some gift. The great Head of the church does not expect the members to serve without a capacity for service. *But to each one is given the manifestation of the Spirit for the common good* (1 Cor. 12:7).

Every believer is bound to believe that he has some spiritual gift, even if he has not discovered it or others think and say that he has none. God says he has, and that settles it. The humblest believer will find God's promise is true if he is willing to wait, work, and pray.

When Dwight L. Moody was examined for church membership, one of the deacons went home and told his family that of all the people whom he had ever examined, young Moody was about the most unpromising. Events proved that God's promises are more reliable than a deacon's judgment.

The spiritual gifts that believers receive are not of their own selection but are such as God chooses to confer upon them. *Distributing to each one individually just as He wills. . . . But now God has placed the members, each one of them, in the body, just as He desired* (1 Cor. 12:11, 18).

No member has a right to be proud of his gifts, any more than an eye has a right to feel superior to the hand or foot. Neither should one member envy another's gifts, seeing that each one has just what God has seen fit to bestow upon him. Each one has more than he deserves and doubtless more than he faithfully uses.

Spiritual gifts are not conferred on us for our benefit but *for the equipping of the saints for the work of service, to the building up of the body of Christ* (Eph. 4:12). Too often, this is forgotten. Many a feeble church has enough unemployed talent in its membership to make it a mighty spiritual power if only its members would exercise their gifts.

1. Many Christians seriously question whether they have any spiritual gift, and the devil encourages them in this belief. So long as he can keep them inactive in the Master's service, they give him little trouble. As a rule, this notion arises from the

fact that they have never attempted any Christian work. They have never tried earnestly to meet any spiritual need, and so they do not know what they can do. A duck would never know it could swim if it did not attempt it.

In the writer's first pastorate, he asked several brethren to lead a meeting during the Week of Prayer. All consented but one. He expressed great willingness but pleaded that he was utterly unable to speak in public. He said his wife and mother agreed that he could not do it. Soon, conversions began to occur, and occasionally, one of the converts was asked to sit on the platform with the pastor and open the meeting. One night, in response to an invitation to accept Christ, an aged woman and her little grandson arose, holding each other by the hand. Their ages were nine and sixty-nine. A few nights later, the little boy was asked to sit with the pastor and lead the meeting. He announced a hymn, read a selection of Scripture, and then prayed. He was small for his age but very mature, and he had a real gift of prayer. He seemed to forget where he was and pleaded so earnestly for the lost that the whole audience was moved to tears. Ungodly men came forward to confess their sins and accept Christ as their Savior. It was the most effective service we had held.

At the close, the brother who thought he had no gift of speech came to me and asked for the privilege of leading the service the next night. If a little nine-year-old could lead a meeting like that, he would attempt it, even if he made a fool of himself. The next night, he led the service in a masterly way, and I never heard him complain again that he had no gift of speech.

It is a great mistake to suppose that all spiritual gifts are necessarily gifts of speech. By no means. What a misfortune it would be if the body of Christ were all a mouth! Let it never be forgotten that the eye, ear, hand, and foot are just as important as the mouth. Romans 12:6-15 shows what a great variety of gifts the Spirit confers on the members of the body. Among them are cheerfulness, hatred of evil, patience in suffering, prayerfulness, and hospitality. The fact is that many spiritual gifts are not recognized as such.

About two years ago, I was at a football game between Yale and Princeton. In the grandstands were nearly twenty thousand people. Directly behind me sat a young lady accompanied by a gentleman. She was one of those healthy, happy girls who carry sunshine with them wherever they go. Whenever a good play was made, she expressed her enthusiasm most cheerfully. Finally, a Yale man caught the ball and, making a fine end run, ran down the field in triumph. Springing to her feet, she threw up her hat, coat, and everything else that was loose and shouted, "Oh, I am so glad I was born."

The young man seemed equally glad, and I am frank to confess that I shared his sentiments. Such splendid enthusiasm! What would it be worth to the cause of Christ? How it would inspire a church, put new life into a dead prayer meeting, or make even drudgery seem delightful.

You may not have the gift of enthusiasm, but perhaps you have the courage to attempt hard things, a patience that never tires, a contagious cheerfulness, the ability to make others see things as you do, or the gift of appreciating other people's good qualities, which is one of the finest of all. You certainly have some gift, for God says so.

2. How can one ascertain what his gifts are? By going to work for Christ. As a rule, no one knows what gifts he possesses until he begins to use them. I was connected with the International Christian Workers' Association a few years ago. This brought me into contact each year with hundreds of Christian workers whom God had signally blessed in some particular way. I

learned the history of many of these people, and the story was practically the same in almost every instance.

They had seen some crying need in their community and tried in vain to get someone else to meet it. Timidly, and in a small way, they had taken up the work themselves. God blessed their labors and gave them such joy and success in the work that eventually they relinquished all other business and devoted their lives to it. Few of them suspected that they had any special gift for the work. They probably would never have known it had they not been moved with compassion for someone's need.

I once wrote a leaflet, "Will You Go Or Send?" It suggested that, as in wartime when men could not go, they often sent a substitute, so the Christian who could not go to the foreign field as a missionary should try to send a substitute. By much prayer and some sacrifice, almost anyone could support one of those native preachers who can be supported for thirty dollars a year. A woman in a destitute part of the West wrote me that she wanted a substitute but was too poor to have one. However, if I would send her some of those leaflets, she would try to interest others, and perhaps they could jointly support one. In a few weeks, she wrote that she had organized a missionary society with a hundred members, which has been supporting native preachers in the foreign field ever since. She probably did not suspect she had the organizing gift but found she did.

I am firmly convinced that if any Christian will take up the first case of spiritual need that presents itself, endeavor to meet it, and continue doing so, it will not be long before he will find that he has a real gift for some spiritual work. He should not complain about his gift and wish it were something else. God knew what He was doing when He conferred it, and if one exercises his gift vigorously and cheerfully, he will find that there is untold joy and blessing to be found therein.

Unless we employ our gifts, they will be taken from us, for

the law which governs all our faculties is this – use them or lose them. In his early life, well-known atheist Charles Darwin was fond of poetry and passionately fond of music. He became interested in natural science and eventually devoted his life to it. In his last years, he testified that his scientific studies had so completely changed his tastes that he no longer cared for poetry, and music caused him positive torture. In other words, he had lost certain gifts by disuse.

Because of this law, it is not strange that Paul so often urges Timothy to stir up the gift that is in him. God forbid that any member of Christ's body should lose his gift and become a near-sighted eye that cannot see very far away, a defective ear that cannot hear heaven's music, or a withered arm that is practically useless.

God forbid that any member of Christ's body should lose his gift.

Finally, let us covet, or, as the Revised Version has it, "desire earnestly" the best gifts. We have no right to envy others' gifts. We must desire for ourselves the best gifts, pray for them, and expect them. There may be a difference of opinion about the best gifts, but I would prefer the gift of prayer. I believe it is a far higher gift than preaching, and I see no reason why this gift is not open to all. Let us all covet it and expect it. *Delight yourself in the LORD; and He will give you the desires of your heart* (Psalm 37:4).

Chapter 5

The Advantages of Personal Evangelism

1. It reaches all classes. *The London Daily News* recently finished a study of more than six months, which showed conclusively that there were over two million nonchurchgoers in that great city. There are 150,000 night workers in New York City, consisting of bakers, cab drivers, and men who work at the newspapers. These people necessarily sleep during the day, and Sunday is no exception. There are also 200,000 men and women belonging to the vicious class who haunt the streets of the same city by night for evil purposes, besides 60,000 homeless wanderers who sit in the parks all night and wait for day to dawn. Of what use is the church to these classes? Who can reach them with the gospel unless he carries it to them directly, by night, and right where they are, in the parks and on the streets? So far as the writer knows, no one is currently doing this night missionary work in this or any other large city in

this country. If you cannot do it, pray that God will raise up consecrated men to do this most needful work.

2. It meets the exact needs of the individual. People are seldom converted by preaching alone. They may be awakened and deeply convicted of sin, but not often do they become personally acquainted with the Lord Jesus without the aid of some individual. Even Saul, to whom the Lord revealed Himself in a unique manner, required the assistance of Ananias before he came into the full light. Cornelius was an earnest seeker of truth, but he had to send for Peter to help him.

The writer talked with three individuals in an inquiry meeting about a year ago. One of them had been deceiving his friends, and duty required him to make certain confessions. He saw his duty clearly but felt unable to do it. Quotations of Scripture and suggestions of various kinds seemed unavailing until finally, I told him the story of the lame man at the gate Beautiful. That story and its application changed his whole attitude and made an almost impossible duty seem a magnificent opportunity. In a moment, he said, "I will do it." A year later, I met him, and he told me how wonderfully God had blessed him, both in the act of confession and in all his work.

The second one was perplexed over some doubtful form of amusement, while the third was facing the question of surrender to Christ.

In each of these cases, the sermon had aroused the conscience and led them to see their duty. However, in neither instance were they quite ready to perform that duty without a further application of the gospel to their peculiar condition.

3. Personal work can be done anywhere. Jesus told the Gadarene demoniac, *Go home to your people and report to them what great things the Lord has done for you* (Mark 5:19). His own

home is the place for every worker to begin. It is often the hardest place of all to do Christian work, but we must be faithful here if we expect the Lord to bless us elsewhere. Paul not only preached the gospel publicly in Ephesus but also went from house to house night and day for three years, warning people with entreaties and tears.

Christian work can be done in connection with one's business. Matthew was converted in a custom house, Moody in a shoe shop, and Peter and John while mending their nets. Mr. S. M. Sayford, the evangelist, was led to Christ in this way. After selling him some goods, a traveling salesman said to him, "I would like to see you a moment in your private office. I have another matter of business which I wish to speak of." When the door

We must be faithful at home if we expect the Lord to bless us elsewhere.

was closed, he took out a little book and showed him a list of names of people who wanted him to pray for them. "Now," he said, "I want you to put your name on that list." Sayford refused. The next time the salesman appeared, he broached the matter again. Finally, Mr. Sayford consented to put his name in the book as one who wanted prayer, and the result was that he was converted. Do not be a coward. Do not be ashamed to speak a word for your Master to your business friends.

One has many opportunities for personal work while traveling. Strangers are more likely to open their hearts to someone who does not know them, and if the approach is tactful, no one needs to fear a rebuff.

Church socials afford a good opportunity to do religious work. Some churches plan events especially for evangelistic work. There is no occasion where the Gospel is out of place. A ball game or a boat race is just as good a place to talk about Jesus as a pulpit or a prayer meeting. The gospel has been confined too often to damp vestries and dreary prayer rooms. It is high time to get it out of doors into the sunlight and divest it of the musty smell and solemn tone that has prejudiced so many people against it. Yes, personal work can be done anywhere, anytime, and by anybody who knows how.

Chapter 6

The Tragedy of a Crown without Stars

If Solomon was right when he said, *He who is wise wins souls* (Proverbs 11:30) and Daniel when he said, *Those who lead the many to righteousness, like the stars forever and ever* (Daniel 12:3), then it follows that every Christian ought to be a soulwinner. Whatever a Christian's occupation may be, it is his business to win souls. Neglect to do it means failure in this life and chagrin and remorse in the life to come.

There is a profound lesson in the story of a lady who died and went to heaven. As she walked the golden streets, she noticed everyone staring at her. At length, this became so annoying that she said to the angel who accompanied her, "Why do the people gaze at me? Is there anything odd in my attire?" "Oh, no," said the angel, "but I suppose you know that there are no stars in your crown." She snatched off her crown, and, sure enough, there was not a single star in it, while all around, as far as she could see, the crowns had stars in them, and some were fairly radiant with stars representing souls won to Christ. She was so grieved that she went to our Heavenly Father and begged to return to earth for a little while, that she might win at least a few stars and not be so conspicuous in heaven. The request was refused. She pled so earnestly that she woke up. It was only a dream.

I am afraid that some of God's children are going through life so thoughtlessly, and, shall I say it, so selfishly, that they will awake in heaven someday to find that there are no stars in their crown and that it is no dream either, but an awful, sad reality.

> *Some are going through life so thoughtlessly that they will awake in heaven to find that there are no stars in their crown.*

One of the saddest persons I ever met was a lady who said to me, "I am the daughter of a minister and a graduate of Wellesley College. I have taught in Sunday School ever since I was fifteen years old. Yet, to the best of my knowledge, I have never led a single soul to Christ."

"I thought that all of your boys became Christians last Sunday."

"That is true, but I had nothing to do with it, and that is breaking my heart."

"Do not be too sure of that," I replied, and then I used an illustration something like this. "Suppose this chandelier was suspended by a chain instead of a rod. Which link in the chain do you think would be the most important one, the first, or the second, or the last one?"

"I do not see why there should be any difference. If you remove any of them, the whole thing would come down."

"Very true," I replied. "Now, in the long chain of events by which God brings any wandering soul back to Himself, tell me which is the most important link, the first, the fiftieth, or the last?"

"There is no difference," she answered. "If any one of the links is gone, you cannot secure the final result."

"Well then, perhaps you did not speak the final words that led your boys to their decisions, but you have certainly spoken many earnest words that prepared the way for someone else to lead them to Christ. Who shall say that your words were not just as important as his?"

"There is some comfort in that, I must admit."

"Certainly, that is why I said it."

"But do you not think that every Christian ought to be able to speak the last words which lead a soul to decision?"

"I do, most surely. I believe that God wishes all His children to be soulwinners and that He has made abundant provision for that end."

"I think something is lacking in myself," she replied.

I thought so, too, and I waited for the Lord to show her what was needed. In a few weeks, she sent a message to me saying that she was now ready to devote her life to the work of winning souls to Christ. She was willing to live in the slums or wherever she could serve God most effectively.

Some people fail through a lack of courage. The secretary of a Young Men's Christian Association told me that he had to let the new men lounge about the place for about a year before it was safe to line them up and say anything about the Christian life. What a moral hero that man must be! I wouldn't have him as a janitor.

With others, it is a lack of faith.

They believe that the gospel is the power of God unto salvation, but they have no confidence that God will save anybody through their use of it. I was spending a Sunday with a certain church and was asked to address the Sunday School. At the close of the service, a dozen or more accepted Christ. About ten days later, one of the deacons came to see me. He said the teachers' meeting was held at his house the week after I was there, and he had charge of it.

He said to them, "I have been doing some thinking this week. You know we have worked here for two or three years without seeing any definite results. We have come to the conclusion that this is a hard town to move and that our school is peculiar. In fact, we have blamed almost everyone except ourselves because we haven't seen the results we hoped to see. You noticed what happened last Sunday. We had a man here who was a complete stranger. He gave a simple, quiet little talk, and you saw what happened in our school, in our peculiar school. Brethren, I have made up my mind that the fault is not with the school nor with the town. The fault is with us. We have beaten the bushes a little and have hoped that the birds would come out and light on our shoulders, but we have not had faith to go in and pick them off the bushes. Brethren and sisters, I think instead of studying this lesson, it would be better for us to kneel down and pray."

They did so, and when they arose from their knees, they began to plan. They decided that they would hold a similar service the following Sunday. As a result, they had more conversions and found so much interest that they decided to hold a series of gospel meetings, which brought a great blessing not only to that church and Sunday School, but to others as well.

Some Christians fail because they are out of touch with God.

As in the case of the young lady already mentioned, we know when something is wrong in our lives that must be made right before we can become an open channel for communicating God's grace. In sending out a circular letter to teachers some years ago, we received several confessions like this. "We are not living so that we can talk to our boys and girls about Christ. Won't you pray for us that we may live so that our testimony shall have some weight?"

This, after all, is the heart of the whole matter. If our life is consistent and our communion with God unbroken, a single word may weigh a ton because all the power of the Holy Ghost is behind it.

I know a pastor who had a teacher in his Sunday School who failed so completely as a teacher that the superintendent had to ask her to give it up. She consented and entered a Bible class as a pupil. Soon, she came to the superintendent and asked if she might teach a class again, provided she found the material for it outside the school. In a little while, her class grew so large that it had to be divided. Still, it grew, and again and again, it had to be divided. One by one, she brought to the pastor's study to confess Christ and unite with the church between fifty and sixty of her scholars.

When questioned afterward about her success and reminded of her failure in the first class, she said, "That first class was my class. I taught it with my own strength and with my own methods. The second class was Christ's class. When a new girl came in, I gave her back to Christ as a mother might her babe. I held her there in the arms of Christ and let Him guide and teach her."

The same pastor had another teacher who, for eight years, at every communion service, brought someone from her class to unite with the church. When we live in such close and conscious fellowship with the Master so that all we say and do is done as His representative, it is easy for Him to pour His grace through us as an open channel. However, when we live a divided life and call Christ "Master" with our lips but crucify Him again and again upon the cross of our own convenience, we may as well take a vacation for a few weeks until we decide once and forever, whose we are and whom we are to serve.

When we live in close fellowship with the Master, it is easy for Him to pour His grace through us.

Conditions of Success in Soul-Winning
– Three Things to Remember

1. The Son of man came to seek and save that which was lost. It was not to start a church, establish a creed, or teach good morals. He came to die for people's sins in order that they might be saved. Furthermore, men are as completely lost now as they were then. Civilization has done away with some of the cruelty and barbarism in the world, but human nature is precisely the same today as it was two thousand years ago. It is thoroughly selfish and sinful, and nothing but the grace of God can make it otherwise (John 3:18, 19; 1 Cor. 2:14; Eph. 4:18).

   No matter how amiable, honorable, and public-spirited a man may be, without Christ, he is lost and needs to be saved. *He who believes in the Son has eternal life; but he who does not obey the Son will not see life, but the wrath of God abides on him* (John 3:36); that is, he is spiritually dead.

2. Remember that the Lord Jesus will save some souls through you if you cooperate with Him. You have some gifts and influence. If you consecrate your gifts and influence to the service of Christ, He will certainly use them to win some of your friends to Himself. While Jesus was in the world, He was the light of the world, but now that He has gone, *You are the light of the world* (Matt. 5:14), and your mission is to so shine as to guide others out of darkness into the marvelous light of God.

3. Remember that Jesus will furnish all the equipment you need. Do you lack wisdom? *For I will give you utterance and wisdom which none of your opponents will be able to resist or refute* (Luke 21:15). Do you lack courage? *Have I not commanded you? Be strong and courageous! Do not tremble*

or be dismayed, for the LORD *your God is with you wherever you go* (Josh. 1:9). Do you lack power? *All authority has been given to Me in heaven and on earth* (Matt. 28:18). Do you lack faith? *The life which I now live in the flesh I live by faith in the Son of God, who loved me and gave Himself up for me* (Gal. 2:20). Jeremiah said, *Behold, I do not know how to speak, because I am a youth. But the* LORD *said to me, Do not say, "I am a youth," Because everywhere I send you, you shall go, And all that I command you, you shall speak* (Jer. 1:6-7). Remember that all your inexperience and inability amount to nothing in the face of the Master's express command: *Follow Me, and I will make you fishers of men* (Matt. 4:19).

Three Things to Do

1. Set the winning of souls before you as a definite aim in life.

An aimless life is generally a useless life. The people who succeed usually set a definite object before them and say, "This one thing I will do, whatever the cost may be." Those who accumulate fortunes or secure political appointments, as a rule, are people who have been bending all their energies in one direction for many years. Why should Christians not set the winning of souls before them as a definite purpose in life? Who is there who could not succeed if he would put the same amount of thought and interest into it that he does into his business? No one expects to succeed in business without toil, patience, and sacrifice. Why should they expect to become experts in soulwinning without similar efforts and sacrifices?

Why should Christians not set the winning of souls before them as a definite purpose in life?

2. Cultivate a passion for souls. David Brainerd, whose

biography ought to be read often by every Christian worker, used to say, "I care not where I go, nor what hardships I endure, if I can only see souls saved. All I think of by day and dream of by night is the conversion of men." Often, he would go into the forest in midwinter, kneel in the snow, and wrestle in prayer until his clothing was wet with perspiration. He often spent the whole night praying for the poor Indians among whom he labored. In almost every such instance, one will find in his diary two or three days after an entry such as this: "Today as I preached the Word, the power of God came down upon those stolid, immovable Indians, and melted and broke their hearts, and swept them into the kingdom by scores."

If anyone says, "I do not have that passion for souls. I am cold and unemotional," let me say for your comfort that it is not a question of what you are by nature but of what you may become by grace. The Lord Jesus was tender and sympathetic, was He not? Well, it is the mission of the Holy Spirit to reproduce in you the life of the Lord Jesus in all its fullness. This includes His principles and feelings, His tender compassion, boundless love, and Heaven-moving faith. All this is your birthright.

3. Begin and continue all your work with prayer. Pray for *all men* (1 Tim. 2:1-4). *I urge that entreaties and prayers, petitions and thanksgivings, be made on behalf of* all men. One advantage of praying daily for each man, woman, and child on the face of the earth is that you never meet a person you have not prayed for many times.

    Make a list of half a dozen or more persons in whom you are especially interested, and make them an object of daily intercession while looking for their conversion. A Sunday School teacher who began praying for his class had the pleasure of seeing eleven young men converted in a few weeks.

Chapter 7

How to Begin a Religious Conversation

Talking is one thing that many people do not consider valuable. It costs so little and is so common that the world does not appreciate its value. However, if our Savior's words be true, that for *every careless word that people speak, they shall give an accounting for it in the day of judgment* (Matt. 12:36), talking is pretty serious business.

It is said of Samuel that *the* LORD *was with him and let none of his words fail* (1 Sam 3:19). In other words, none of them were lost, but all found their way to their proper destination, did their appointed work, and returned laden with blessing to the God who gave them.

In the Savior's prayer in John 17, He says, *I glorified You on the earth, having accomplished the work which You have given Me to do* (John 17:4). Accomplished! Finished! Not a word left unsaid, not a deed left undone, of all God gave Him to do. How unfinished and incomplete do our lives seem in comparison.

Talking is a very potent agency for good. When we see how persuasive and forceful some men are in presenting a business proposition or how eloquent they are in pleading a political cause, we cannot but wish that their talents were consecrated to the service of Christ. Furthermore, whatever one may think about women speaking in a church meeting, certainly outside of the church, women have a fluency and fervor that would make them valuable allies of any cause they might espouse.

> *When we see how eloquent some are in pleading a political cause, we cannot but wish that their talents were consecrated to Christ.*

A single word, fitly spoken, has often changed one's whole career. Said a noble man, "If I have been happy or useful in the world, it is due largely to a chance question from a stranger. I was a poor boy and a cripple. Watching a ball game one day with envious feelings, a man at my side said to me, 'You wish you were in the place of those boys, do you not?' 'Yes, I do,' was the answer. 'I reckon God gave them their money and health to enable them to be of some use in the world. Did it ever occur to you that He gave you your lame leg for the same reason, to make a man of you?' I did not reply, but I could not get his words out of my mind. My crippled leg is God's gift, to teach me patience and strength! I did not believe it, but I was a thoughtful boy, and the more I thought about it, the more I was convinced that the stranger had told the truth. It worked on my temper, my thoughts, and, finally, my actions. The idea has sweetened and blessed me all my life. I wish I could find the man who gave me this password, which has led me to the source of all good."

Christian conversation seems to be almost a lost art in some places. How seldom does one hear the subject broached in homes or at a dinner party, even when all the people present are professing Christians! Riding on the train with a stranger one day, I began talking about religion. After a while, he admitted that he was a church member. "If that is the case," I said, "why didn't you talk to me like a Christian and not compel me to work so long to find out your position?" "People don't do that down our way," said he. "If I should speak to a man who came into my store about religion, what do you suppose he would think of me?" "He would probably think you were a Christian," I replied. "Well, no one talks about religion down our way, not even the ministers. We never hear from them on the subject except from the pulpit."

That Christians do not talk more about the things of the Kingdom is a constant surprise to the unsaved and often an occasion of doubt. Said a skeptical lady to a friend of mine, "I will tell you why I am a doubter. I was in a sewing society last week. Forty ladies were present, and everyone was a church member except me. I was there for three hours. We talked of everything down to crazy patchwork, but not a word about Jesus. I cannot believe that they see in Jesus Christ the beauty or power that you speak of. I am convinced that there is a great deal of sham in the profession of Christian people."

On the other hand, it is refreshing to meet those who are evidently in the same condition as Peter and John, who said, *We cannot stop speaking about what we have seen and heard* (Acts 4:20). A gentleman driving along overtook a stranger and invited him to ride. As he approached him, he said to himself, "I wonder what the man is thinking about and what subject of conversation he will introduce. Surely, it will be one of three things – the weather, the crops, or the election." It was none of these. His first words after the usual salutations were, "How is religion down in your country?" The question startled the man by its directness, but it showed where the other's heart was and led to a long and profitable conversation on heavenly things.

How much might each of us accomplish if our hearts were warm and glowing with love to Christ, and our minds were on the alert to improve every opportunity that God sets before us?

While no one can deny that it requires tact and skill to carry on a religious conversation successfully, is it not worthwhile to study the art until we become proficient? If we follow Paul's advice to the Colossians, we will always have something to say. If we begin each day with David's prayer, *Let the words of my mouth and the meditation of my heart be acceptable in Your sight, O LORD, my rock and my Redeemer* (Psalm 19:14), we shall keep in touch with God. If we watch for souls as those that must give an account, we shall have opportunities enough so that, in a short time, we shall find Christian conversation a real pleasure to ourselves and a blessing to others.

How to Begin a Religious Conversation

Open it just as you would any other conversation. Decide what you wish to say, and then say it. Say it in the same tone you would speak of anything else. It is a great mistake to suppose that one must lower his voice and look solemn when he introduces the subject of religion. The gospel is good news. If you do not think so, the less you say about it, the better, but if it is genuinely good news to you, then speak of it in the same joyful, hearty way that you would bring any other glad tidings.

If the gospel is genuinely good news to you, then speak of it in the same joyful way that you would any other glad tidings.

The president of one of our largest theological seminaries was led to Christ in this way. During his college course, as he came out of class one day, a classmate slapped him on the back and said, "Say, Gus, I wish you were a Christian." Gus made no reply, and the matter was dropped, but years later, he told his friend that remark had led him to accept Christ as his Savior. The hearty and natural way his companion spoke made him feel that he was missing something he could not afford to lose.

1. Study the art of diverting a conversation to spiritual topics. Go through the Gospel of John and carefully study the Savior's methods of approaching men. Indeed, the Gospel of John might well be called the personal worker's Gospel since it is so full of incidents that illustrate this important subject. Take the case of the Samaritan woman. Jesus asked her for a drink of water. As He drank it, you can imagine Him saying, "This is very good water, but anyone who drinks it will soon thirst again; whosoever drinks of the water that I shall give him shall never thirst, but the water that I shall give him shall become in him a well of water, springing up unto eternal life." "What is that?" asked the woman. "A water, which if you once drink it, you never thirst again." "Sir, give me this water that I thirst not, neither come all this way to draw." By this clever device, He excited her curiosity to attract attention to Himself. At other times, He was the Bread of Life, the Vine, the Door, the Good Shepherd. Whatever the subject of conversation, He always left His hearers face to face with the Son of God and His supreme claim upon them.

"But I am not the Savior," you reply. "Very true, but if you are a Christian, the Savior dwells in you, and He has said, *For I will give you utterance and wisdom which none of your opponents will be able to resist or refute* (Luke 21:15).

I know a lady to whom a salesman was trying to sell an article for taking out stains. He was rubbing away and meanwhile eloquently describing the merits of his goods. Soon, the lady said, "I know something that will take out stains, too." "What is that?" asked the man eagerly, not knowing whether some other dirt-killer had canvassed the town ahead of him.

"The blood of Jesus Christ which cleanses us from all sin, do you know anything about that, my friend?" Do you suppose that man would demonstrate his goods again for six months without thinking of that "other something" that could take stains out of a sinful heart? I doubt he ever forgot that lesson.

A friend of mine at the Northfield Conference was asked by a delivery man to direct him to a certain man's tent. "I am very sorry," he replied, "I cannot tell you where to find him, but if you had asked me the way to heaven, I could have told you. Do you know the way to heaven?" "No," said the man, "I cannot say that I do." "Well, it is just this way," said my friend, and he went on to explain it. The result was that the man was led to Christ right then and there. Indeed, that was an easy way to open religious conversation. Anyone could do that. You could do it.

Do not suppose this was the first time he had used this little device. On the contrary, he was always using it. Studying the most effective ways of turning a conversation to Christ had become a habit of his life. If a stranger asked him the time of day, he would likely answer, "It is a quarter past ten, just the time of day for a man to be saved, if he isn't already. How is it with you, my friend? Are you a Christian?"

Of course, such a question might seem a little abrupt, and it certainly would be unexpected. However, it is pointed and pertinent and calls for a definite answer. Whatever the result might be, the interview would not soon be forgotten.

A Salvation Army girl was selling *War Crys* in a saloon when a man said to her, "You don't believe in the Bible, do you?" "I do," said the girl, "or I wouldn't be in this place, I can assure you." "You don't mean to say you believe that story about the whale swallowing Jonah?" "Certainly I do; God says so, and I believe it." "Nobody believes that story nowadays." "Well," said the girl, "when I get to heaven, I will go to Jonah and ask him if he had a real experience in a real whale." "But you won't find Jonah in heaven; he isn't there." "Then suppose you ask him," said the girl quietly, assuming that if Jonah was not in heaven, he might be in the other place.

"That girl was bright," you say. Very true, but who gave her that wit and wisdom? The Holy Spirit, who will give you all the wit and wisdom you need for the work to which He has called you. *The anointing which you received from Him abides in you, and you have no need for anyone to teach you* (1 John 2:27). If Christians would only believe what God says, they would have more confidence to engage in personal work.

2. Choose an opportune time and place. It is not a good idea to stop one who is running to catch a train to inquire about his soul. Neither is it the highest wisdom to give a hungry man a tract. It is far better to give him a cup of coffee and make it so hot that he cannot drink it. Then, while he is sipping the coffee, you can perhaps say something to warm his heart.

It is a good plan to put people under some slight obligation. If your neighbor on the bus has no paper, buy one, and after glancing at it, pass it to him, saying, "Would you like to see the morning paper?" After he has read it, the most natural thing is to open a conversation about the day's news, and from this, you can move to more important topics.

People are often more ready to talk with strangers about religion than with those they know. The Holy Spirit is convicting people of sin. The providence of God is continually softening hearts and preparing the way for someone to drop in the good seed of the gospel. Remember also that thousands of people have never once in all their lives had the way of salvation made plain to them and then, in a firm but loving way, have been urged to settle the question and settle it now.

3. Watch for souls as those that must give account. When an insurance agent is introduced to a man, his first thought is, "How old is that man, and how much life insurance does he carry?" He usually is not long in finding out, either. A friend was accosted by the words, "Shine your shoes, boss?" Looking at his feet, he said, "Well, **I** guess I do need a shine, but I didn't know it. How did you know that my shoes needed a shine?" "That's my business, boss. When a man comes into this hotel, I don't look to see what kind of hat he wears. I don't look at his face. I just look at his feet. That's my business, you see." So it should be our business when we meet a man to think of his soul and the possible ways of helping him.

It should be our business when we meet a man to think of his soul and the possible ways of helping him.

Do not always walk home from church the same way and with the same person. Join someone who is not a Christian, and as you walk along, express your views about the sermon and see what impression it made upon him. That is what sermons are for, in part, to give people something to talk about and arguments to use in leading people to make a decision.

4. Use gospel cards and tracts to open a conversation.[1] One of the great secrets of success in personal work is to have something to give away. By this means, you can always secure the attention of an individual or a crowd. It is easy to pass out a little card saying, "Would you like something to read?" After it is read, the reader's mind is on the subject you wish to introduce, and you lose no time in getting at it.

---

1   Excellent, attractive tracts can be purchased at low costs from https://mwtb.org

Chapter 8

To Whom We Should Speak

There is no rule of universal application, but one must consider the age, sex, and general condition of those he approaches.

Uncle John Vassar's Rule

Uncle John Vassar was accustomed to speaking to everyone he met on the subject of religion, but his rule might not be the best one for all. He was a man of years and experience and could hold his own with people whom a younger person could not so successfully deal with. On one occasion, he accosted two ladies in a hotel in Boston and inquired if they were Christians. "Certainly," they replied.

"Have you been born again?" he asked.

"This is Boston," said the ladies, "and you know that we do not believe in that doctrine here."

Uncle John opened his Bible and showed them what God had to say about the subject, and in a short time, all three were on their knees. When her husband returned at night, one of the ladies told him about her encounter with Uncle John.

"I wish I had been here," said the man.

"What would you have done?" asked his wife.

"I would have told him to go about his business."

"But, husband, if you had been here, you would have said he was about his business."

That was a true estimate of Uncle John Vassar. He made it "his business" to witness for Christ always and everywhere. Let us make it our business to witness for the Master at all times and places. It may not seem best to speak to everyone we meet, but we should at least be willing to do so if God requires it. Whether He does or not can usually be determined by asking Him.

Mr. Moody's rule

When Mr. Moody was beginning to do Christian work, he committed to speak to at least one person on the subject of religion every day for a year. He kept his promise faithfully until the last day of the year. As he was about to retire that night, he remembered that he had not spoken to anyone that day on the all-important question. It was rather late, but he did not wish to break his record. So he rushed out into the street and, hailing the first person he met, inquired if he was a Christian. The man told him it was none of his business and added other remarks that were not altogether complimentary.

Mr. Moody returned to his room thinking he had made a fool of himself and had probably hurt the cause he had meant to help. One of his friends who heard of the incident rebuked him sharply and told him that he must stop speaking to people so abruptly, or he would make himself obnoxious.

God evidently took a different view of the matter, for in a few days, the man he addressed so abruptly sought him out and apologized for how he had responded. He told him that he had had no peace since that night on account of his sins and asked him to show him the way of salvation. If we listen to the devil, he will tell us that any kind of Christian work is foolish. Let us listen to God alone.

Begin at Home

It is so much easier to speak to others than to those of our own household that they are liable to be overlooked, but we certainly have a duty at home that we cannot afford to neglect. If our life has been inconsistent, we had better confess it frankly before we talk to others about their life. If we wait until we are perfect before we begin, we shall never begin. Remember that all God's work is done by imperfect workmen.

Do not omit to speak to the children of Christian parents, ministers included. Too often, they have been so busy looking after other people's boys and girls that their own have been neglected. We are often mistaken in assuming that those who live in Christian homes must necessarily be Christians.

> *We are often mistaken in assuming that those who live in Christian homes must be Christians.*

Surely, all of our schoolmates, shopmates, and friends have a right to expect of us a real interest in their spiritual welfare. It is not wise to talk to them constantly about religion, but we should let them know how we feel and that they are always on our hearts, even if we only speak to them occasionally.

Speaking to Strangers

Perhaps the greatest perplexity arises here, but let us never forget that we have an infallible Guide who is sufficient for all emergencies. Ask Him when in doubt, and He will quickly let you know if He wishes you to commend Him to a stranger.

Sometimes, the Spirit impresses us so strongly that He leaves no doubt about our duty. A friend was walking along a crowded street with his mind so occupied that he did not notice whom he passed. Suddenly, he felt an irresistible impulse to speak to someone. He looked up and saw a man standing by a lamppost. He said, "My friend, are you a Christian?" "No," said the man, "but I have hardly slept for two nights thinking about this very matter." It was very easy, of course, to lead that man to Christ.

As a rule, the Spirit speaks to us through our judgment, which is a vehicle of God's thoughts as truly as our conscience. The opportunity of speaking to a stranger, and the fact that you may never see him again, is a call that one ought to consider prayerfully. If we ask for help, God will suggest some way of broaching the subject, and we can usually soon tell whether the person is willing to talk with us. If he shows any interest, we can follow it up, but if he is silent and refuses to talk, it is probably better to pass on to a more congenial topic.

Chapter 9

How to Diagnose the Case

I n dealing with a person, we must first find out where he stands. It is important to know whether he is interested or indifferent, whether he has doubts or difficulties that really trouble him, or whether he is justifying himself by his good works or the faults of others.

If he has gone into an inquiry room or remained to meet afterward, it is perfectly proper to ask if he is a Christian. You can say, "I hope you are a Christian," or something which will draw out an expression of opinion. If the person is a stranger whom you have met outside of a religious meeting, you can enter into a conversation on some general topic and rapidly lead up to the subject of salvation. It is surprising how soon an opportunity will occur for the main question when one is prayerfully seeking to be led by the Spirit.

While riding through the country with a pastor, the writer

came to a house where the town's poor were kept. An old man came hobbling up from the barn, and the following conversation occurred:

"Where are you going, my friend, when you move away from here?"

"I don't know, I'm sure."

"I should suppose that you would go to the place they are preparing for you."

"What?" he said, with a look of surprise.

"I understand that they are building a fine home for you, and I should think you would want to move into it when you leave here."

"What do you mean?" he asked with great eagerness.

"Well," said I, "the good Book says, *In my Father's house are many dwelling places; if it were not so, I would have told you; for I go to prepare a place for you. If I go and prepare a place for you, I will come back and receive you to Myself, that where I am, there you may be also* (John 14:2-3). If I were you, I would plan to move into my new home when I left this poorhouse."

"Oh," said he with a smile, "you mean heaven."

"Certainly," I replied.

"Well," said he, "I hope I shall go to heaven."

"Of course you do, but what reason have you for thinking you will go to heaven?"

"I think good people are going that way."

"That is true, but they do not go to heaven unless they have a title to one of those homes. Have you secured your title?"

"No," said he sadly, "I have not."

"Would you like to secure it?"

"Yes, of course I would."

"You can get it right here if you wish. I am authorized to issue those titles."

"I certainly would like to get one if you can tell me how."

"The Bible says, *All of us like sheep have gone astray, each of us has turned to his own way* (Isaiah 53:6).

"Does that apply to you, my friend?"

"Yes, I have had my own way right along."

"The Bible also says, *Let the wicked forsake his way and the unrighteous man his thoughts; and let him return to the* LORD, *and he will have compassion on him, and to our God, for he will abundantly pardon* (Isaiah 55:7). Are you willing to repent of your sins and call upon God for mercy?"

"Yes, sir, I am."

"Are you willing to give up your own way and henceforth walk in God's way?"

"I am."

"Jesus says, *Here I am! I stand at the door and knock. If anyone hears my voice and opens the door, I will come in and eat with him, and he with me* (Rev 3:20). You hear His voice. Are you willing to open the door of your heart and invite Him to come in and take possession of your life?"

"I am."

"Do you here and now accept Jesus Christ as your personal Savior?"

"I do," said he solemnly.

"Will you shake hands with me as a pledge *of* it?"

"Yes, sir," and he did so most heartily.

"Very well," said I. "Now let us tell the Lord just what you have told me. Take off your hat." He did so, and I removed mine, and we had a few words of prayer. Then, I gave him a little covenant to sign and keep as a reminder of what he had promised the Lord and what the Lord had promised him. The pastor had joined me by this time, and we drove away. It was a seed sown by the wayside, and all I could do was follow it with prayer.

From that day, the old man managed to get down to church each Sunday, though it was several miles away, and he was quite lame. Soon, he came before the church and asked for admission on his confession of faith, passing a good examination.

Doubtless, there are many who, like this man, are out of the Kingdom not wholly on account of sin but partly on account of ignorance. They do not know how to get in. They want to be saved, but no one has ever made the way of salvation plain to them and then definitely asked them to accept Christ as their personal Savior. They are waiting for some Philip to cross their pathway and lead them to Jesus.

Others, perhaps, have had an invitation and have refused it. They were not willing to accept Christ then, but now they are. Great changes have occurred. Their *There are many who want to be saved, but no one has ever made the way of salvation plain to them.* home has broken up, and their dear ones taken away. One after another, their earthly props have been removed until now, sad and lonely, their hearts are hungry for the comfort and fellowship which only Christ can give. They always needed a Savior, but they did not realize it. Now, they realize it but do not know how to find Him. Who will make the way of salvation plain to them and lead them to Jesus?

On another occasion, I handed a small card to a man asking if he wanted something to read. On it, he saw the word Christian, and at once, he said with a sneer, "'Christian,' yes, I have neighbors who are Christians, and I have some who are not, and the latter are more neighborly and more honorable in business every time." "That may be," I said, "but remember that it is not their religion which makes your neighbors mean and dishonorable, but the lack of it, and it is not fair to blame Jesus Christ for what does not belong to Him."

Then I added, "It may be that you do not feel the need of a Savior now, but the time will surely come when you will feel it."

"I guess I need Him enough now. My wife died about a year

ago, and then I lost my daughter. My home is broken up, and I haven't anything left to live for."

The man's voice trembled, and the tears began to come. I saw that I had touched a tender chord, and I said, "My friend, if anyone on this earth needs Jesus Christ, I think you are the man." Then I held up Christ as a comforter and told him how willing Christ was to come into his sad heart to make it glad and into his desolate home and make it bright with heavenly hopes. Then, taking it for granted that he did not know how to find Christ, I explained the way of salvation. Then I said, "Now, my friend, with this understanding of what it is to become a Christian, are you willing to accept Christ as your Savior right here and now and give me your hand on it? "Yes sir, I am," he replied, and he grasped my hand heartily. Then we removed our hats. I prayed, and he prayed, after which he gave me his name and told me all about himself. This was at a county fair in the middle of noise and confusion. Horses were racing, the carnival hawkers were shouting, and the merry-go-round was in full blast. Amid that noisy crowd, this man with a bared head confessed his sins to God and invited Jesus Christ into his heart.

A great aid in opening a conversation with strangers is to have a variety of leaflets or gospel cards with you. You can hand one to someone, saying, "Would you like something to read?" If he does not express an opinion, you can give him another, saying, "This one is a little different," or "Here is one I think you will enjoy." By this means, you gradually become acquainted, give him one which plainly presents the way of salvation, and ask him if he has accepted Christ as his Savior.

One of the most common conditions we find is profound ignorance of what the Christian life is. One day, the writer gave a card to a lady sitting with him on the train. She seemed interested, and so he gave her another and another. Then he asked if she was a Christian. She replied that she did not know.

"But you would know if you were asked whether you were American or French?"

"Certainly."

"What is your idea of the Christian life?"

"I suppose that if I tried as hard as I could to do right, I should be a Christian."

"Is that what the Bible teaches?"

"I do not know."

"Would you like to know?"

"I certainly would."

He then gave her another tract entitled, "Only Three Steps Into the Christian Life." She was ready to take those three steps then and there and went on her way rejoicing.

Sitting in a hotel in Denver, I was reading a newspaper. By my side sat a young man talking with two others. Soon, he uttered an oath. Taking out a little card entitled, "Why Do You Swear?" I laid it down on the arm of the chair between us and went on reading. He picked it up and read it. As soon as his companions left, he said to me, "My friend, that is the best thing on swearing I have ever seen. I know it is an awful habit, and I ought not to do it, but you see, I am a newspaperman on the *Chicago Inter Ocean*. I am thrown in with a rough crowd, and I cannot seem to overcome the habit." He then went on to tell me about himself, and we had a long heart-to-heart talk. Remember, he began the conversation, and he did most of the talking. I simply laid down the little card and improved the opportunity when the way opened.

The following incident shows the importance of making a correct diagnosis. I was asked to speak to a certain man in an inquiry meeting at Northfield. Before I could reach him, another worker talked with him, so I turned to others. Later, I saw the worker leaving him, and approaching him, I said, "Have you settled the great question?" "No," said the worker, turning back, "this young man is going away unsaved because he will not give his heart to God." "What is the trouble?" I inquired and sat down beside him. I soon surmised that it was not a case of stubborn unwillingness to yield to Christ but rather a lack of confidence in his ability to make the surrender real. He was like a general who was willing to surrender but who questioned his ability to make his soldiers lay down their arms. I told him that if he would surrender, Christ would enable him to make the surrender good. I then suggested that we kneel and that he follow me sentence by sentence while I led him in prayer. He said that he did not know whether he could honestly do it. "Follow me as far as you can, and then stop," I replied. He consented to do that, and we knelt together. I led him in a commitment to Christ as strong and complete as I knew how to make it, going cautiously at first but making it stronger as I saw his willingness to follow. When we arose, he told the first person he met that he had accepted Christ as his Savior. So far as I could judge, the first man who talked with him failed because he had made a false diagnosis of the case, mistaking the man's lack of confidence in himself for stubborn willfulness.

When we have ascertained one's actual position, the next thing is to lead him to accept Christ.

The main object is not to lead people to give up their bad habits, attend church, or even join the church, but rather to accept Christ as their personal Lord and Master. We should then show them from God's Word that they have forgiveness of sins and eternal life (Acts 10:43; John 3:36).

They should also be instructed in the duties of the Christian life, especially the duty of confessing Christ publicly and the habit of daily prayer and Bible reading.

Chapter 10

The Importance of Tact

Tact has been described as the art of putting ourselves in another's place. It is a work of imagination, but if we have little or no imagination, we must cultivate it to succeed in winning men. The reason for putting ourselves in the place of others is that we may know their needs and so supply them, their purposes and so persuade them, their prejudices and so conciliate them.

To do this successfully, we must study the condition of those we would help and imagine how we would think and feel if we were in their condition. If we have had any experience in their line of work, it will help us. If not, we can sometimes acquire the requisite knowledge by reading. When Bishop Whittle was called to a mission near the railroad yards, he asked an engineer how to reach the railroad operatives. The answer was, "Read 'Lardner's Railroad Economy' until you can ask an engineer a question and not make him think you are a fool." He won the hearts of the first railroad men he addressed by asking them whether they preferred inside or outside connections. After discussing connections, steam heaters, and exhausts, he invited them to his chapel, and every man came the following Sunday.

It is a great help in dealing with people to make them feel at ease. If they make a blunder, skillfully divert attention from it, making theirs seem less conspicuous. A story is told in Washington of the wife of a senator. A plain man, a constituent of the senator, called and was invited by the lady of the house to have a cup of coffee. The cups were of very delicate French china and very fragile. The plain man, unaccustomed to such wares, broke a cup. It was an annoying incident and might have been quite embarrassing to him, but the lady with splendid tact instantly crushed another cup in her slight fingers, saying as she did so, "It is wonderful how easily these cups break." The plain man was heard to say afterward, "Do you suppose that there is anything I would not do for that woman or her husband?"

It is not wise usually to talk to people about their relation to Christ in the presence of others. It embarrasses and may anger them. However, one can often tell an appropriate story and thus indirectly accomplish the same end without offending anyone. Dr. Talmage's account of his conversion illustrates tactful preaching in the presence of others. An old evangelist named Osborne stayed one night at his father's house. As the family sat by the fire, he said to the father, "Are all your children Christians?"

"Yes, all but DeWitt."

"He did not turn to look at me [Talmage] but gazed into the fire and quietly told a story of a lamb that was lost in the mountains on a stormy night. Everything in the fold was warm and comfortable, but the poor lamb perished in the cold. He did not make any application. If he had, I would have been mad. I knew I was the lamb and could not get any peace until I found Christ."

The writer was once working at a county fair. In front of the platform provided for the singers and speakers were a large number of seats for the audience. We had an organ, a chorus, and three large megaphones. The latter would carry the sound of the singing half a mile, and people on the race course were soon drawn away by the new attraction. At first, the people stood aloof from the seats and refused to occupy them. They had never seen a religious service at a fair and were suspicious. Noticing this, the leader ordered the singers down from the platform, directing them to scatter about in the seats. As soon as the crowd saw that there were no explosives under the chairs, they crowded in and filled them. Then, the leader recalled the singers to the platform, having used them as decoys to attract the people to the chairs. There was no deception about this. The people were timid and suspicious, and it was necessary to show them that there was nothing to be afraid of and to fill enough of the seats so that they would not make themselves conspicuous by sitting down. A church audience that favors the back seats can usually be beguiled to the front by arranging with a few people to fill the first two or three pews each night before the audience arrives.

Paul says, *I have become all things to all men, so that I may by all means save some* (1 Cor. 9:22). Though he was entitled to support, he worked with his own hands making tent cloth by night, in order not to be a burden to the churches, but set an example of generosity to other believers. In this way, he doubtless gained the sympathy and respect of other laboring men. On one occasion, when he had been arrested at Jerusalem and was being carried off to prison, he asked for the privilege of addressing the crowd. To the surprise of the people who supposed him to be a mischief-making foreigner, he began by saying he was a Jew and addressed them in their own language. By this tactful introduction, he gained their attention and held it while he told them the wonderful story of his conversion.

His epistle to Philemon is probably the most tactful letter ever written. It is an affectionate message from an old friend who once led him to Christ and who has now met and led to Christ one of his fugitive slaves, Onesimus. It is also a wise and effective plea that Philemon should forgive and receive back the penitent slave. The letter contains sixteen reasons why Philemon should grant Paul's request, and he must be a hard man indeed who could refuse such a request.

Evil can often be effectively rebuked if it is done tactfully. A gentleman crossing the ocean was much annoyed by the profanity of several men. Finally, he said to them one day, "Gentlemen, I believe all of you are Englishmen, and if so, you believe in fair play, do you not?"

"Certainly, that is a characteristic of Britons everywhere."

"Well, gentlemen, I notice that you have been indulging in a good deal of profanity, and I think it is my turn to swear next. Isn't that fair?"

"Of course it is," said the others.

"Very well. Remember that you are not to swear again until I have had my turn."

"But you will not take your turn?"

"I certainly will just as soon as I see a real occasion for it."

True love is blind to many little faults. However, it is also eager for one's salvation.

Occasionally, they urged him to use his prerogative, but he assured them he would just as soon as there was a good reason. All this was done in a playful bantering way, but the result was that he kept their profanity bottled up all the rest of the voyage and doubtless compelled them to realize the folly and sin of swearing.

If we are conscious of a lack of tact, let us ask for it, for the promise is, **My God will supply all your needs** (Phil 4:19). The basis of true tact is a love that shrinks from putting another in an embarrassing situation, and we should always remember this in dealing with inquirers. True love is also blind to many little faults. However, it is also so eager for one's salvation that it misses no opportunity to press home his urgent need for a Savior, and the Savior's supreme love for him.

Chapter 11

How a Sinner May Get Right with God

Centuries ago, Job asked the question, *How can a mortal be righteous before God?* (Job 9:2). In all ages, the moral sense of mankind has been raising the same question. Many answers have been given:

1. The heathen answered it this way. "Make an offering to the gods sufficient to compensate for the wrong done." So they brought presents of fruit and flowers, gold and silver, and sometimes they even offered their own children as a sacrifice to the gods. They were always looking for some way of pleasing God without right living. The heathen method is still a favorite one, even in Christian lands. Many a man serves the devil all his life and then builds a library or endows a hospital to atone for his sins.

2. Others say a sinner can get right with God by keeping

the commandments. Three things are to be said about this method:

a. Keeping the law does not atone for past sins. If one were to obey God's law perfectly from this time on, that would not atone for the sins of the past.

b. The law was never designed to save men from sin but only to show them they are sinners. When Mr. Moody's boys were quite young, he said to one of them, "I am going down to the field, and when I return, if you will have on clean clothes, and if your face is clean, I will take you out for a ride." The little fellow ran to his mother at once and had his face washed and his clothes changed. Before his father returned, however, his face and clothes were soiled again. When his father arrived, the boy claimed the promised ride, but he said, "Ah, my boy, I promised you a ride on condition that your face and clothes were clean, but they are not." "Oh, yes," said the boy. "They must be clean for mamma put on fresh clothes and scrubbed my face with soap and water." As the boy insisted, the father took him in his arms and, carrying him into the house, held him up before the mirror and let him look at himself.

He used the mirror to show the boy that his face was not clean, but he did not use the mirror to wash his face, did he? No, he used water for that. The Decalogue is God's mirror to show man that he is a sinner, but it cannot save him from sin. It requires grace to do that.

c. No one ever kept the law of God perfectly except the Lord Jesus Christ, *for all have sinned and fall short of the glory of God* (Rom. 3:23). This method of getting right with God is an utter failure.

3. Paul's answer to the question is this: justification through faith in Christ. *Even we have believed in Christ Jesus, so that we may be justified by faith in Christ and not by the works of the Law; since by the works of the Law no flesh will be justified* (Gal. 2:16).

Since man has broken away from God by sin, it is evident that if any reconciliation is made, the overture must come from God since man has nothing to offer.

When God told Abraham to take his only son Isaac and offer him as a sacrifice on Mount Moriah, the aged patriarch obeyed instantly. He even arose "early in the morning" and set out on his sad journey. When they reached the appointed place, Isaac said to his father, *The fire and wood are here, . . . but where is the lamb for the burnt offering?* Abraham answered, *God will provide for Himself the lamb for the burnt offering, my son* (Gen. 22:7-8), and God did.

> **If any reconciliation is made, the overture must come from God since man has nothing to offer.**

So, in all ages, the moral sense of mankind has been searching the universe for some adequate atonement for sin. The best they could find did not satisfy their own sense of justice. The position of the heathen world without the Bible is this, "Lord, this is the best we can find. We know it is not suitable or sufficient, but what can we do? Behold the wood and the fire, but where is the lamb for a burnt offering?" Revelation answers, *God will provide for Himself the lamb for the burnt offering,* and He has, even the Lamb of God who takes away the sin of the world. *But He was pierced through for our transgressions, He was crushed for our iniquities. . . . All of us like sheep have gone astray, each of us has turned to his own way; but the LORD has caused the iniquity of us all to fall on Him* (Isaiah 53:5-6).

This, then, is the Scripture method of getting right with God: justification through faith in Jesus Christ. *God was in Christ reconciling the world to Himself, not counting their trespasses against them* (2 Cor. 5:19). Notice also that Christ's death and not His life is the ground of our reconciliation. *Much more then, having now been justified by His blood, we shall be saved from the wrath of God through Him* (Rom. 5:9).

Our Unitarian acquaintances are fond of talking about the beautiful life of Jesus. However, the life of Jesus alone is a discouragement to the sinner because he has no power to reproduce that life were it not for His death. Jesus Christ might have gone about saying beautiful things and doing good until this day, but had He not made atonement for us by His death, we should still be burdened with the guilt of sin. Not in the manger, on the mount, nor in the garden was our atonement made, but on the cross. *He Himself bore our sins in His body on the cross* (1 Pet. 2:24).

Three things are to be remembered:

1. By the death of Christ, we are delivered from the guilt of sin.

2. By the life of Christ in us, we are delivered from the power of sin.

3. By the coming of Christ, we shall be delivered from the presence of sin.

What Is Justification?

The word justify means to reckon or declare righteous. Forgiveness is a negative term, meaning to put away or remit. Justification is a positive act and means not simply forgiving the sinner or letting him off from the punishment he deserves but declaring him righteous (Rom. 4:5).

How can God reckon one righteous who is not righteous? This is a fair question, and we must face it. Suppose a merchant in a small town has fallen into debt. He is not a good buyer, he is not accurate in his accounts, and he is shiftless. Suppose a rich uncle who has made a fortune in the same business and has retired should visit him. After a few days, he says to his nephew, "John, I hear bad reports about you; people say that you are sadly in debt and that your credit is poor. I have had a good year and believe I can help you. If you will add up all your debts, I will give you a check for the whole amount."

John accepts his offer and pays off his creditors. As they leave his store, they say to one another, "We are fortunate to get our money this time, but we will not trust him again. He is the same shiftless John and will soon be as badly in debt as ever." Now, what has his uncle accomplished for John? He has paid his debts, but he has not restored his credit.

Suppose on the other hand that the uncle had said, "John, I have been out of business a few years, and I find that I am getting rusty. I like this town and have about decided to partner with you." John is delighted, of course. The uncle says: "I will put in my capital and experience, but I shall insist upon being the business manager. You can be the silent partner and work under my direction. And John, I think you had better take down that sign over the door, for your name does not command the highest respect in this town. Suppose you put up my name, instead, with '& Co.' I think it will look better, and you can be the company."

John gladly complies with the conditions, and the business opens under new management. John goes out to buy goods, and what does he find? Instead of refusing to trust him, every merchant in town is glad to give him credit because his rich uncle has become identified with the business. In the one case, the uncle paid his debts but did not restore his credit. In the other, he restored his credit by going into partnership with him.

God's law says that the soul which sins shall die. When Jesus took our place on the cross and died for our sins, He paid our debt. However, He did not restore our credit or make us righteous. Had there been no resurrection of Jesus, we could not have been justified, although it is conceivable that we might have been forgiven. When Jesus rose from the dead and identified Himself with us by faith, coming into our hearts and taking possession of our lives, He not only paid our debts but restored our credit. He made it possible for God to declare us righteous since we have gone into partnership with a righteous Savior who has not only kept the law perfectly Himself but who can help us keep it. He is the managing partner, and we simply obey His orders. We have even taken down the old sign, and now we bear His name – Christian.

Martin Luther said, "If anyone knocks at the door of my heart and inquires if Martin Luther lives here, I should reply, 'Martin Luther is dead, and Jesus Christ lives here.'" Paul had the same idea, for he said, *It is no longer I who live, but Christ lives in me* (Gal. 2:20). *For you have died and your life is hidden with Christ in God* (Col 3.3).

When a woman marries, she loses her name and identity, but she takes her husband's name and shares his rank. If he is a duke, she becomes a duchess. If he is a prince, she becomes a princess. Even so, the believer who surrenders his life to the Lord Jesus loses his identity and sins but shares His name, character, and rank with Him. God calls him Christian because he is the bride of Christ, His only begotten Son. God can justly declare him righteous because he is forever united to One who is righteous and who is able to make him like Himself.

> *God can justly declare the believer righteous because he is forever united to One who is righteous.*

If Jesus lived a holy life in one body, He can surely do it in another if that body is yielded to His control. God then can properly and justly reckon the believer righteous because of his union with the righteous Savior who has atoned for his past sins by His death on the Cross. He can guarantee his present and future conduct because that life has been committed to His keeping.

He is able also to save forever (Heb. 7:25) and *able to keep you from stumbling* (Jude 24). If He guarantees to present us before the presence of God's glory absolutely faultless, surely God can safely reckon us as righteous. The ground of our justification then is not what we are, but whose we are, not our own good works or our desire to be righteous, but our union with the Lord Jesus, *who was delivered over because of our transgressions, and was raised because of our justification* (Rom. 4:25).

Chapter 12

What Is Conversion?

Since Jesus says, *Unless you are converted and become like children, you will not enter the kingdom of heaven* (Matt. 18:3), it is important that we know just what conversion is. Let us first consider some things that are not conversions but are often mistaken for them.

To improve one's life is not conversion. It is a common opinion that if one drops all bad habits and cultivates good ones, reads the Bible, and goes to church, he can, in a short time, make himself a Christian. That is a mistake. The Christian life is not simply an improvement of the old life but a different kind of life altogether, namely a life of obedience to Christ. Suppose you had a sour apple tree, which you wished to convert into a sweet apple tree. What would you do? Would you dig about it, prune it, and scrape the bark? No, indeed. A hundred years of such improvement would not make the tree bear sweet apples, but introducing a graft from a sweet apple tree would do it very quickly. Even so, a lifetime spent improving one's habits does not make one a Christian, but the entrance of Jesus Christ into the heart by surrendering the will does it in a moment. People do not become Christians by improving their lives but by accepting Christ. *He who has the Son has the life; he who does not have the Son of God does not have the life* (1 John 5:12).

Conviction of sin is not conversion. One may feel a keen sense of guilt on account of his sins, but if he does not confess and forsake them, there is no conversion. I heard a man say that he was convicted of sin twenty years ago by hearing a street preacher in San Francisco. All that time, he had carried the burden of guilt until about three months before when he accepted Christ, and his burden rolled away. For twenty years, he had been convicted of sin, but he had not been converted.

A compromise with God is not conversion. Sometimes, when people are convicted of sin, they try to make deals with the Almighty. A young man told me that on being awakened, he decided to take up every Christian duty except that of confessing Christ. Much to his surprise, he could find no peace or assurance of forgiveness. Indeed, he was more miserable than before. Finally, he made a public confession of Christ as his Savior, and the peace of God came into his heart at once. It is not enough to obey Christ in part, but we must wholly yield our will to Him if we expect to be saved.

It is not enough to obey Christ in part, but we must wholly yield our will to Him if we expect to be saved.

What is conversion? The word convert means "to turn about." As applied to spiritual things, it means a turning of the soul to God. *All of us like sheep have gone astray, each of us has turned to his own way* (Isaiah 53:6). The real essence of sin is this: the sinner is determined to have his own way. It may not be the worst way in the world. It may not be an immoral or vicious way, but it is his way and not God's way, which he ought to follow. The only course for the sinner to pursue is to turn about, abandon his way, and accept God's way. *Let the wicked forsake his way and the unrighteous man his thoughts; and let him return to the LORD, and He will have compassion on him* (Isaiah 55:7). Conversion then is a turning of the soul to God, a surrender of the will to the Divine will, and an acceptance of Jesus Christ as our Lord and Master.

The effects of conversion. When the sinner, realizing the folly of further resistance, finally surrenders his will to the Lord Jesus, a great change occurs. God forgives his sins and so changes his heart that henceforth, he loves God's way better than his own. *I will give you a new heart and put a new spirit within you; . . . I will put My Spirit within you and cause you to walk in My statutes* (Ezek. 36:26, 27). The sinner no longer has a controversy with God. The great question of life is settled, and henceforth, his aim is to know and do the will of God. Though he may fail and come short of his purpose again and again, as long as he recognizes Jesus Christ as his Lord and Master and honestly strives to obey Him, he is a converted man.

Man is not perfect, but he is on the way to perfection. He cannot overcome the habits of a lifetime in a moment, but he recognizes a new power in his life, even the power and presence of the Lord Jesus Christ. With His help, he can conquer his besetting sins and build up a Christian character, for He is not only *able to keep you from stumbling, and to make you stand in the presence of His glory blameless with great joy* (Jude 24).

Influences leading to conversion. The Word of God is a very effective agency. It is like a mirror in which the sinner sees himself as he really is. That is why Christ bids us preach the gospel to every creature because there is life in it. *The word of God is living and active and sharper than any two-edged sword* (Heb. 4:12). One can hardly read the Bible continuously and not realize that he is a sinner and needs a Savior.

The Holy Spirit and Providence also cooperate with the Word, as in the following instance. A businessman in Brooklyn was hurrying to catch the ferry when the gate shut down before him. Instantly, the words flashed into his mind: "And the door was shut." He said to himself, "If that had been the door of heaven, it would never have opened for me again." "And the door was shut, and the door was shut" kept ringing in his ears. He went to his business but could not pay attention to his work. Finally, he went home and told his wife about the morning incident, and together, they knelt and gave their hearts to God.

Personal influence is also a mighty factor in leading people to a decision. Our testimony has weight with them if our lives are consistent. Our prayers and entreaties are often more effective than we think, and even a look or a touch of the hand at the right moment has often led a hesitating soul to decide for Christ.

Distinction between conversion and regeneration. On one occasion, a man said to me, "From the preaching which I heard in my boyhood, I was led to suppose that when one became a Christian, he needed to go through some extraordinary process called a change of heart or regeneration. This book that you loaned me teaches that what is required is simply a change of purpose. Now, please tell me which is right and which is wrong?" I replied, "They are both right. You could not change your heart if you tried. You could not make it love what it naturally hates, could you?" "No, I suppose not," he said. "But you could change your purpose, could you not? Could you decide to obey the Lord Jesus?" "Certainly," he replied. "Well," said I, "if you will change your purpose and accept Christ as your Savior, God will change your heart and cause you to love what you once hated and hate what you loved." "Is that all there is to it?" said he. "Certainly," I replied. He lost no time in accepting Christ, and God gave him a new heart.

Our testimony has weight with others if our lives are consistent.

When is the proper time for conversion? Behold, now is "the acceptable time," behold, now is "the day of salvation" (2 Cor. 6:2). If you say, "I want more time to think about it," I answer, "What will you gain by waiting? What have you gained by waiting already? No, friend, what you need is not time but a decision. You know you are a sinner, and Christ is the only one who can save you. The simple question is, "Will you accept Him as your Savior?" God expects you to do it and commands you to do it. If it is to be done, you are the one who must do it. Will you do it, and will you do it now?

Chapter 13

What Is Meant by the New Birth

Nicodemus was a good man and an earnest seeker after truth. For this reason, he came to Jesus by night so that he might have an uninterrupted interview. He acknowledges the divinity of Jesus, and though an official teacher of the Bible himself, he humbly takes the place of a disciple. If I am not mistaken, this was his attitude: "Teacher, I have many rules and precepts by which I govern my life, but when I hear you speak, I feel as if I know nothing. O, Teacher, tell me your rule for holy living! Tell me all you know!"

The Master replied, "Nicodemus, you are trying to save your soul by good works, by fasts, gifts, and sacrifices. This is not the way. What you need is not new rules but a new heart, not learning but life, and life always begins with birth. *Unless one is born again he cannot see the kingdom of God* (John 3:3)."

What the New Birth Is Not

It is not an improvement of the old nature. The Bible represents human nature as hopelessly bad and incurably sinful.

It is blind: *That we should look upon Him, nor appearance that we should be attracted to Him (Is. 53:2).*

It is wicked: *The heart is more deceitful than all else and is desperately sick* (Jer. 17:9).

It is at enmity with God: *The mind set on the flesh is hostile toward God* (Rom. 8:7).

It is dead: *And you were dead in your trespasses and sins* (Eph. 2:1).

This is human nature, as God describes it. It is not capable of improvement, and God does not attempt it. For it does not subject itself to the law of God, for it is not even able to do so. *Not subject to the law of God, neither indeed can be* (Rom. 8:7). When a bell has been cracked, it gives out a hoarse, guttural sound, which is very annoying. You may bind it with hoops and bands, but nothing will restore the clear, sweet tone. The only remedy is to return it to the factory, melt it down, and recast the bell.

Man is a bell made to sound the praises of God. However, sin entered and cracked the bell, and now man sounds his own praises instead of the praise of God and does his own will instead of God's will. No amount of good works or pious resolutions can restore a heart ruined by sin. The only remedy is to take it back to God, who made it, and let Him make it over. *Unless one is born again he cannot see the kingdom of God* (John 3:3).

Man is a bell made to sound the praises of God.

What Is the New Birth?

It is the imparting of a new nature, which is Jesus Christ. *I will give you a new heart and put a new spirit within you* (Ezek. 36:26).

I have a friend who has six acres of greenhouses. A large part of his business is the culture of roses. He imports the wild stock from Ireland because it is peculiarly hardy. He does not put the wild rose bushes into the greenhouse just as they are and cultivate them. If he did, he would only obtain wild Irish roses, which are not worth ten cents a thousand. The first thing he does with the wild stock is to graft it with buds from the choice roses, which he wishes to produce. Then he places it in the greenhouse and uses all the appliances known to modern flower culture. The result is those elegant General Jacque and American Beauty roses, which are in high demand.

Man is like the wild rose. He cannot produce the fruit of the Spirit because there is no Holy Spirit in him until Christ has been accepted. Neither can he forgive his sin nor effectively resist its power. God's way is to impart unto him a new Divine nature that can overcome sin and produce the fruit of righteousness. That divine nature is Jesus Christ. When one has accepted Him, he becomes a child of God and is said to be born again. *But as many as received Him, to them He gave the right to become children of God* (John 1:12).

How Is the New Birth Brought About?

By believing God's Word. Man was lost by doubting God's Word; he is saved by believing it. *Born again not of seed which is perishable but imperishable, that is, through the living and enduring word of God* (1 Pet. 1:23). *Born again not of seed which is perishable but imperishable, that is, through the living and enduring word of God* (2 Pet. 1:4).

The Results of the New Birth

1. An immediate deliverance from the guilt of sin. *Therefore there is now no condemnation for those who are in Christ Jesus* (Rom. 8:1).

2. A consciousness of Divine sonship. *Because you are sons, God has sent forth the Spirit of His Son into our hearts, crying, "Abba! Father!"* (Gal. 4:6).

3. A love for other Christians. *We know that we have passed out of death into life, because we love the brethren* (1 John 3:14).

4. The believer finds that he actually loves God's will better than his own, though he may not always do it.

5. He begins to exhibit a likeness to Christ. As children resemble their earthly parents, so one who is born of God increasingly resembles his Elder Brother. *And everyone who has this hope fixed on Him purifies himself, just as He is pure* (1 John 3:3).

Sometimes, this resemblance appears in a very sudden and striking way. At the close of a service, I was introduced to a young lady who had been noted for her frivolity and flirting with young men during the service. As I began talking, she looked at me with an expression that seemed to say, "Talk if you will, but I do not propose to be influenced by what you say." Soon, there was a change of expression, and she said, "I will do it." "Do what?" I said, for I had not asked her to do anything. "I will accept Christ as my Savior." "Very well," I replied, "suppose we kneel and tell the Lord just what you have told me." We knelt together, and I prayed. Then she prayed and burst into tears. When she dried her eyes, she suddenly left me and left the door. When she returned, I found that she had gone out to ask those young men with whom she had been flirting to come in and do what she had done – give their hearts to God.

Ten minutes before, so far as I could judge, she did not care whether anyone was saved, least of all herself; but within ten minutes, the Spirit of Him who came into the world to seek and to save the lost had so taken possession of her that she did what I think all will agree was a very hard thing to do. What was this but the family resemblance, showing itself immediately and strikingly?

6. As soon as Christ enters, a conflict begins, for the old nature is no better than it was before. *For the flesh sets its desire against the Spirit, and the Spirit against the flesh* (Gal. 5:17). If we yield to the flesh, we shall sin, but it is possible to live a life of continual victory. *But I say, walk by the Spirit, and you will not carry out the desire of the flesh* (Gal. 5:16). *For sin shall not be master over you* (Rom. 6:14).

When an egg is laid, in the midst of the white fluid floats a little germ of life, which, though invisible, contains the chick to be. Day by day, during the process of incubation, the germ of life grows, and the white fluid disappears. Soon, the chick emerges from the shell, and the white fluid is all gone.

So when one is born of God, the Christ-life enters and coexists with the self-life. As Christ is formed within us by the Spirit, there ought to be less and less of self and more and more of Christ until finally Christ reigns completely, and self is dead and gone. As someone has said, death is the breaking of the shell, when we step out into Paradise, from darkness into light.

> *As Christ is formed within us, there ought to be less and less of self and more and more of Christ.*

Those who are born only once must die twice (Rev. 20:6).

Those who are born twice do not die at all but simply fall asleep (John 11:26).

Chapter 14

How to Introduce a Man to Christ

In the conversion of Nathanael, we have a good illustration of the principles involved in leading a person to Christ.

1. Every believer has a message to the world. *Philip found Nathanael and said to him, "We have found Him of whom Moses in the Law and also the Prophets wrote – Jesus of Nazareth, the son of Joseph"* (John 1:45). Philip did not talk about himself but about Jesus. That is what we should do. That is what we were called into the kingdom for—to talk about the King. The world is prejudiced against Jesus Christ. Sin has blinded their vision, and they do not see Him as He is. They think He is unreasonable and exacting, and they see no beauty in Him that they should desire. Our business is to reveal the beauty of the Son of God, so they will feel their need for Him.

When Ole Bull, the great musician, visited this country, he

found an old friend from his boyhood in Philadelphia, John Ericson, the great shipbuilder. They had a delightful interview, and as he was leaving, Ole Bull handed out some tickets to a concert and invited his friend to come and hear him.

Ericson declined and, when pressed for his reason, frankly confessed that music was torture to him and begged to be excused. Of course, nothing more could be said, but Ole Bull decided to compel his friend to hear him somehow. A few days later, he appeared at Ericson's office with his violin and asked Ericson if he had any skillful mechanics. He said he had an accident with his violin and needed a little help. Ericson touched a button, and when a man appeared, he asked him to send Mr. B_____ to the office. When Mr. B_____ presented himself, Ericson told Ole Bull to explain to him what he wanted done. In a few minutes, the man returned with the repairs made. The great musician took the violin, drew his bow across it a few times to see if it was in tune, and then glided into one of those matchless melodies that only Ole Bull could evoke from an instrument. Instantly, every clerk in the office dropped their pens. Ericson lay down his paper and began to listen, and all the men in the factory gathered around the open door. There, they stood spellbound for twenty minutes until the music ceased. When he laid down his bow, Ericson cried out, "Go on, go on, my friend. I never knew before that I had a capacity for music."

The poor, sinful world has the same idea about Jesus that Ericson had about music. They think they do not need Jesus and should not enjoy Him. You and I know better, and it is our business to interpret the needs of their hearts, portray the beauty and sweetness of Christ's character, and make them hungry for Him. Every believer has a message to the world, and the better he knows Christ, the stronger his message will be.

2. Every believer in bearing His message to the world is sure to meet with controversial inquiry. *Nathanael said to him, "Can any good thing come out of Nazareth?"* (John 1:46). There was only one word in Philip's testimony that one could find fault with, and that was the word, Nazareth. Nathanael, good man as he was, could not avoid the temptation to criticize, and he seized the opportunity immediately. "Nazareth," he said, "the most disreputable town in all Galilee. Can any good thing come out of Nazareth?" Human nature is bound to find fault with God's message. When Jesus spoke to Nicodemus about the new birth, he inquired haughtily how a man could be born when he was old. When He told the young lawyer that he must love his neighbor, he was willing to justify himself and asked, "Who is my neighbor?" When Jesus spoke to the Sadducees about the resurrection, they brought up the old story about a man with seven wives and wanted to know who would be first in the kingdom.

> **Human nature is bound to excuse itself even if it has to blame others.**

It was just this way in the Master's day, and it will always be the same. Human nature is bound to excuse itself even if it has to blame others. If you study these excuses carefully, I think you will find they are all included in three classes.

1. Objections relating to the Bible or the doctrines it teaches, such as the inspiration of the Scriptures, the Trinity, the atonement, the doctrine of forgiveness, etc.

2. Objections based upon the inconsistencies of Christians.

3. Objections that relate to themselves in some way, such as, "I am not very bad," "I am afraid that I cannot hold out," "Sometime, but not now."

3. Every believer, in meeting the world's objections, has a sufficient answer. *Philip said to him, "Come and see"* (John 1:46).

If you study this subject, you will see what a complete answer this is to any possible objection. Suppose that one is uncertain about the authority of the Scriptures. Let him come and see. That is, come to Jesus and see what He thinks about the question, and His opinion ought to be final. He evidently regards the Pentateuch as the work of Moses and the various chapters of Isaiah, which he quotes as the Word of God through His servant Isaiah, and Jonah as a real character who had an experience such as is attributed to him by the record bearing his name.

If one doubts the possibility of forgiveness, let him come and see. Let him kneel down and confess his sins, and he can demonstrate the thing in a very short time.

If he insists that he is not very bad, let him come to Jesus Christ and see; let him line up alongside the spotless Son of God and see whether or not he is bad.

Jesus actually guarantees to save everyone who commits the keeping of his soul to Him.

If he is doubtful about holding out, let him see what the Savior thinks about the matter, for He alone must do the saving. He finds at once that Jesus not only thinks that He can save him but that He actually guarantees to save everyone who commits the keeping of his soul to Him (Heb. 7:25; Jude 24; 1 Cor. 10:13).

4. As soon as the believer begins to bear His message to the world, Jesus draws near. *Jesus saw Nathanael coming to Him, and said of him, "Behold, an Israelite indeed, in whom there is no deceit!"* (John 1:47).

Let us never forget that as soon as we begin to speak to a sinner, a third party draws near, and He does not make a crowd either. This third party is invisible, but He makes Himself heard, illuminating our feeble words to make them mighty to the pulling down of the strongholds of sin. *I will give you utterance and wisdom which none of your opponents will be able to resist or refute* (Luke 21:15).

5. As soon as a sinner begins to talk with Jesus, the light begins to come. *Nathanael answered Him, "Rabbi, You are the Son of God"* (John 1:49).

By all means, get an inquirer on his knees as soon as possible. He can see many things there which he cannot see standing. If he is not accustomed to praying, and most people are not, ask him to follow you sentence by sentence as you lead him in prayer. In this way, you will be sure that he confesses his sins and invites Christ to come into his heart and take possession of his life. You can also pledge him to daily prayer, the confession of Christ to the world, and anything else that may seem best. When you rise from your knees, question him and see if he knows that he is saved. Do not leave him until he is assured of it, not because he feels happy, but because God's Word assures him of his salvation.

Chapter 15

How to Deal with Excuses

"I Am Not Very Bad"

The mistake that this man is making is judging himself by a false standard. The remedy is to correct his standard. Say to him, "It may be that you are not very bad in your own estimation or in the opinion of others, but let us see what God says about you. His Word is the only true standard."

Open your Bible and ask him to read aloud Romans 3:10. THERE IS NONE RIGHTEOUS, NOT EVEN ONE. After he has read it, ask him a few questions:

"Whose words are these which you have read?"

"God's words."

"Does He know the real condition of a man's heart?"

"Yes."

"Does He know a man's heart better than the man himself?"

"Probably."

"Who does He say is righteous?"

"He says that there is none righteous."

"What, not one?"

"No, not one."

"Are you an exception to this rule?"

"I suppose not."

"Then you admit that you are not really righteous?"

"I suppose I must."

Ask him to read Romans 3:23. Then say to him, "Who does God say have sinned?"

"All have sinned."

"Are you an exception?"

"No."

"Then you admit that you have sinned and come short of the glory of God?"

By this time, the man is becoming uneasy. He is beginning to realize that whatever he may be in his own estimation, in God's sight, he is a sinner. You have withdrawn his attention from the inconsistent church members with whom he has formerly compared himself, and you have fixed his mind upon the great God to whom he must give an account and by whose holy law he must be judged.

Another good verse to use with this class is Isaiah 53:6. After the man has read it, ask him, "Who does God say has gone astray?"

"All of us."

"Does that include you?"

"I suppose it does."

"What does He say we have done?"

"Each of us has turned to his own way."

"Then, according to God's Word, having one's own way is sin?"

"So it seems."

It is well to emphasize this point strongly, for, to the average person, the word "sin" means some form of vice or crime. According to this verse, however, the real essence of sin consists in having one's own way instead of walking in God's way. It may not be an immoral way, a dishonest way, or an untruthful way, but it is his way and not God's way in which he ought to walk.

Returning to the verse, you can ask, "What do you say of a sheep which has gone astray?"

"It is lost."

"Then, if you have had your own way through life instead of doing God's will, you too are lost, are you not?"

"So it appears."

"Admitting then that you are a lost sinner, what does God say that He has done with your sins?"

"And the Lord has caused our iniquity to fall on Him."

"Then your sins have made it necessary for Jesus to die on the cross?"

"Yes."

"When Jesus took your place on the cross and died for your sins, you refused to acknowledge Him as your Savior, did you not?"

"Yes."

"And you have never once thanked Him for what He has done for you, have you?"

"No."

"And yet you say you are not very bad. If this is not bad, will you tell me what is? There is only one thing worse, and that is to continue rejecting such a Savior."

In dealing with self-righteous people, it is well-nigh useless to argue. Neither would it be a very gracious thing to tell them that you thought they were great sinners. They would not believe it if you did, and they might likely retort, "And you are another."

Bring self-righteous people face-to-face with God and make them realize that they are dealing with Him rather than with you.

The only effective way of dealing with them is to bring them face-to-face with God and make them realize that they are dealing with Him rather than with you. If you have sufficient time, it is good to ask a person to read the fifty-third chapter of Isaiah, using the first personal pronoun. *He was despised and forsaken by me, A man of sorrows and acquainted with grief; And like one from whom men hide their face He was despised, and we did not esteem Him. But He was pierced through for my transgressions, He was crushed for my iniquities; The chastening for my well-being fell upon Him, And by His scourging I am healed. I like sheep have gone astray, I have turned to my own way; But the LORD has caused my iniquity to fall on Him.*

Another way is to ask a person if he knows that he has committed the greatest sin a man can commit. He will probably answer, "No, I have not." Ask him to read Matthew 22:37, 38. Then ask him what is the greatest sin. He will answer that violating the first and greatest commandment must be the greatest sin. Ask him if he has kept that commandment. When he confesses that he has not, hold him to the point until he admits that he is guilty of committing the greatest sin that a man can commit, namely, that of not loving the Lord his God with all his heart and soul and mind.

"I Am Afraid I Cannot Hold Out"

In dealing with any case, it is good to determine the cause of the man's condition first and then look for a cure. There may be many causes, but whatever they are, there is always a sure cure in the Word of God. In this case, it is evident that the cause of the man's fear is this: He is thinking of saving himself instead of committing the case to Christ. He means to try a little harder than ever before to do good, but he has failed so often in the past that he has little confidence that he will succeed any better in the future. The man is right. He certainly will fail if he relies upon his own efforts to lead a Christian life.

In this case, the remedy is to take the man's attention away from himself and fix it upon the Lord Jesus, who alone can save him. Say to him, "My dear friend, the question is not whether you can hold out but whether God can save you. Let us see what He says about it." Opening your Bible, ask him to read Hebrews 7:25 aloud. *Therefore He is able also to save forever those who draw near to God through Him, since He always lives to make intercession for them.* After he has read it, say to him, "If God is able to save anyone who draws near to Him, there is certainly some hope for you. With the salvation such as Christ offers, there are no hopeless cases, do you see?"

"Yes, it does look a little more hopeful, I must confess, but I am afraid I would fail, if I started in the Christian life. My persistence is not very strong, and I am easily discouraged."

"That may be true, but do you know the Savior has made provision also to keep you from falling? Read what He says in Jude 24." *To him who is able to keep you from stumbling and to present you before his glorious presence without fault and with great joy.*

"Isn't that splendid? 'Able to keep you from stumbling, and to present you without fault.' Blameless would mean a great deal, but without fault means much more. That is the condition in which Christ promises that you shall be when He presents you before the Father. Moreover, the joy referred to in that verse is not the joy of the sinner, though that will be unspeakable, but the joy of the Savior as He looks with actual pride upon His finished work. It does not seem possible, does it, that you can be saved so completely and made so perfect and beautiful that the Lord Jesus will put you on exhibition as a sample of His handiwork, with actual pride and joy? And yet that is precisely what He says He can do, and He certainly ought to know. Now does not your case seem hopeful, looking at it from God's standpoint?"

"Yes, I must admit that it does, but you see, my case is peculiar. I had a grandfather who was a drunkard, and I have inherited from him an appetite for liquor. Occasionally, an awful craving for strong drink comes upon me with irresistible power, and down I go before it. That is the real cause of my apprehension. If it were not for that, I think I could be saved, but you see, my case is peculiar."

"Yes, I see your case is peculiar, but do you know we have a peculiar Savior? In the first place, He was acquainted with that grandfather of yours and knows all about that appetite. In the second place, He has made ample provision for it in the Book. Indeed, He has provided a special promise for just such cases. Read, if you will, 1 Corinthians 10:13, *No temptation has overtaken you except what is common to mankind. And God is faithful; he will not let you be tempted beyond what you can bear.*

"Now let us sum it all up. Jesus says that if you commit the keeping of your soul to Him, He is able to save to the uttermost and keep you from falling. Furthermore, knowing just how weak you are, He guarantees that no temptation shall be allowed to come to you that you cannot bear. When temptation does come, as come it must to all. He will provide some door of escape. But this is not all. He promises that He will present you before God so faultless and perfect that He Himself will be proud of you. Now, what will you do? Will you keep trying to save yourself and fail as you always have, or will you commit your soul to this Savior who can save, keep, and protect you from every foe?" If the man is sincere in his desire to be a Christian, there is only one alternative. Usually, he will accept it.

If these verses do not lead a person to a decision, I have sometimes tried this method: "You are lost now, anyway, are you not?" "Yes, I am lost now." "Well, if you should try the Christian life and fail, you could not be any worse off than you are now, could you?" "No." "But if you should succeed, you would be a great deal better off, would you not?" "Certainly." "Then it looks to me as if you have everything to win and nothing to lose by starting, is that not so?" "Yes, but I never thought of that before." "Will you then kneel right here and commit the keeping of your soul to Christ?" "I will."

I have seldom found a person who could not be convinced by such simple reasoning if they honestly desired to be a Christian.

Dealing with Those Who Say "Not Now"

As usual, let us consider first the cause and then the cure. Perhaps some habit must be abandoned, some companion must be dropped, or some unpleasant duty must be done. It may be only the natural inertia of the soul that shrinks from grappling with a subject so serious, but more likely, there is some secret sin that the man is unwilling to abandon. The real cause is that the man is not willing to surrender his will to God. He wants his own way, and though he flatters himself that he will yield to God sometime, he is not willing to do it now.

Whatever the cause, the cure is always the same – God's Word. Ask the man by whom he expects to be saved if he is ever saved. He will answer, "God alone can save me." Emphasize that thought by having him read aloud John 6:44, *No one can come to Me unless the Father who sent Me draws him.* Call his attention to

God's Command

Acts 17:30, God *is now declaring to men that all people every-where should repent.* After he has read the verse, ask him if God has a right to make such a command. Ask him if he, who is dependent on God for salvation, dares to refuse to obey this plain command. Show him the consequences of such a refusal. Proverbs 1:24, 26, 28, *Because I called, and you refused, I stretched out my hand and no one paid attention; . . . I will also laugh at your calamity; I will mock you when your dread comes, . . . Then they will call on me, but I will not answer; They shall seek me diligently but they will not find me.*

God's Time

2 Cor. 6:2, *Behold, now is "the acceptable time," behold, now is "the day of salvation."* Show him that God's time is the best and only sure time. There is no certainty that he will be accepted tomorrow, but there is a positive promise for today. Make him realize that the habit of putting off his responsibility will grow constantly stronger and that ten years from now, he will be less disposed to repent than he is today. Show him that there must be some moment of definite surrender to God and that no lapse of time will make that surrender any easier. Indeed, it will grow harder as the years pass by, and if he puts it off, the chances are that he will never do it.

The Uncertainty of Life

Proverbs 27:1, *Do not boast about tomorrow, For you do not know what a day may bring forth.* Show him that in putting off repentance, he is reckoning upon the continuance of life, which is entirely uncertain. Remember that Satan is persuading him in his subtle way to wait a little longer. The old serpent does not dare suggest that he never repent or even that he put it off a long time, but he cunningly says, "Not now."

Occasionally, a soul may be won by taking the devil's side of the argument and pleading his cause so boldly that the absurdity of his reasoning is apparent. A friend of mine at a

Northfield conference was asked to speak to a young man with whom many had labored in vain. Meeting him alone one day he said to him, "These people in the hotel are bothering you a good deal on the subject of religion, are they not?" The man blushed and admitted that he had been somewhat annoyed. Then followed a conversation something like this.

"You don't need to give any thought to this matter for a long time yet. You had better put it off for at least a couple of years, don't you think so?"

"I am not sure it would be well to put it off so long as that." "Why not?" "Because I might not live two years." "That is true. Well, put it off one year. That is safe enough, is it not?" "No, I don't suppose it is entirely safe, for I might die in one year." "Sure enough, you might. Well, put it off six months. Are you willing to do that?" The young man hesitated. "Call it three months. Will you promise not to think of it for three months?" "I wouldn't like to promise that." "Why not?" "Because I might die in three months." "Will you promise not to think of it for a week? That is safe enough, isn't it?" "No one can be sure of a week, I suppose." "You are certainly sure of one day, aren't you?" "No, not positively sure of even one day." "Well," said my friend, "if you are not sure of even a single day, hadn't you better give your heart to the Lord now?" And he did, right then and there.

It pays sometimes to interpret Scripture with a watch, as in the following instance. One day, a Christian worker met a man with whom he had often talked on the subject of religion. Asking him when the question was to be settled, he received the answer, "Very soon, I think."

"If you wish to be saved, what do you have to do?" "Accept Christ." "Just so, but when?" "Now, I suppose." "Yes," said the worker, "that is just what the Bible says, and now means Now." Taking out his watch, he said, "It is just three o'clock. Will you at three o'clock this afternoon accept Christ as your Savior?"

After a long struggle, he replied, "I will." Off went their hats, and there in the street, they praised God for the grace of decision. At a meeting that night, the convert was the first to pray, and this is what he said, "Lord, I thank You for saving me at three o'clock this afternoon."

Dealing with Those Who Complain of Christians

In dealing with those who complain of the hypocrites in the church, it is helpful to open your Bible to Matthew 7:1 and ask them to read it. *Do not judge so that you will not be judged.* Also show them Romans 14:12. *So then each one of us will give an account of himself to God.* Then ask the objector, "Who has appointed you judge over your fellow men? Has the Lord appointed you?"

"No."

"Have your fellow men selected you for this important position?"

"Of course not."

"You don't mean to say that you have appointed yourself judge, do you? A self-appointed judge! Who ever heard of such a thing!"

Then, ask him to read Romans 2:1. *Therefore you have no excuse, everyone of you who passes judgment, for in that which you judge another, you condemn yourself; for you who judge practice the same things.*

Ask him if it ever occurred to him that he was a hypocrite himself, and when he answers in the negative, say to him:

"Well, let us see. You condemn the hypocrites because they pretend to be what they are not?"

"I do."

"But when you claim that the reason you are not a Christian is because of the hypocrites in the church, you are pretending what is not true. The real reason why you do not become a

Christian is because you want your own way and are not willing to obey God. When you say it is because of the hypocrites, you are saying what is not true, and you know it."

Show him John 21:21, 22. *So Peter seeing him said to Jesus, "Lord, and what about this man?" Jesus said to him, "If I want him to remain until I come, what is that to you? You follow Me!"*

Say to him: "Admitting that there are hypocrites in the church, what is that to you? If every man in the church were a hypocrite, that would not excuse you from the duty of repentance."

"If there was a call for volunteers to defend this country, would you stay out of the army because some bad men would probably enlist?"

"I suppose not."

"Possibly you are a Mason or an Odd Fellow. Are there any black sheep in your lodge?"

"I must confess that there are a few."

"And yet you joined the lodge, knowing this fact. Do you urge others to do the same?"

"That is true."

"Why, then, do you offer such a silly excuse when the subject of religion arises? If you do not wish to be a Christian, say so in a manly way, but do not try to hide yourself behind the faults of others. The only safe hiding place for a sinner is the cross of Christ, and you will realize it someday."

The only safe hiding place for a sinner is the cross of Christ.

A man once said to his pastor that the reason why he did not accept Christ was because he once had a partner who was a professing Christian who wronged him in business.

"That is your real reason, is it?" asked the minister.

"It is," replied the man.

"Suppose we put it down in writing," said the minister, and drawing out his notebook, he wrote: "The reason why I am not a Christian is that my partner, who claimed to be a Christian, wronged me in a business deal."

Tearing out the leaf, he folded it and handed it to the man, saying, "When you come before the Great White Throne and God asks you why you have rejected His Son, just hand Him that paper," and turning away, he left him. Hardly had he reached home when his doorbell rang, and there stood the man, with the paper in his hand.

"Well," said the minister, "what can I do for you?"

"I have brought this paper back. I am afraid it would not answer as an excuse to give to God."

"You think that God would not accept it."

"I am afraid not."

"We may as well tear it up then," and the minister tore it into fragments and threw them away.

"Now have you any other excuse which is better?"

"I can't think of any."

"If you do not have any good reason for not becoming a Christian, should you not give your heart to God now?"

"Yes, sir, and I will."

Among the tracts I referred to is an excellent one for the people who are always complaining about the hypocrites in the church. On one side is the question, "Do those hypocrites hinder you?" On the other side is the following:

"Remember, when the church goes through the Pearly Gates, those hypocrites will be left outside the gate, on your side, unless you repent, and you will have to spend all eternity with them. Would it not be better to repent and live with them a few years in the church than to spend all eternity with them elsewhere? You must spend some time with those hypocrites somewhere. Where shall it be?"

If one scatters these freely, all the excuse-makers in town will close their mouths forever on the subject of hypocrites.

Chapter 16

Doubts and How to Dispel Them

I t is not strange that men are doubters. Sin has so blinded our moral vision that we do not see the truth as it is but in a distorted fashion, which makes it less attractive. *But a natural man does not accept the things of the Spirit of God, for they are foolishness to him; and he cannot understand them, because they are spiritually appraised* (1 Cor. 2:14).

Furthermore, the truth as it is in Jesus carries with it the condemnation of the sinner, and no one enjoys reproof or rebuke. As the lawyer, willing to justify himself, said, "Who is my neighbor?" so the natural heart questions the authority of the Bible and even the existence of God rather than confess its sin. Add to this the fact that the devil, who first injected doubt into man's mind and is rightly called by our Savior the father of lies, is ever seeking to prejudice the creature against his Creator. It is not strange that all thinking people pass through a period of doubt about the fundamentals of religion, and some are so completely blinded that they never come out of their spiritual darkness.

In dealing with doubters, it is important to determine their real position. Some skeptics are mere triflers who are too lazy to grapple with the truth in a determined way and find it easier to doubt and drift with the current of their natural inclinations. Others use their skepticism as a cover for an ungodly life. You can say to such when they question the inspiration of the Bible that one proof of its divine origin is the fact that it describes their condition so completely and tells how they came into that condition. Naturally, they will wish to see the passage, and you can show them 2 Corinthians 4:4. *And even if our gospel is veiled, it is veiled to those who are perishing, in whose case the god of this world has blinded the minds of the unbelieving so that they might not see the light of the gospel of the glory of Christ, who is the image of God."*

Remind them that to doubt the Bible does not alter the facts which it reveals, but it does subject them to the charge of making God a liar (1 John 5:10) and puts them under condemnation. *He who does not believe has been judged already, because he has not believed in the name of the only begotten Son of God. This is the judgment, that the Light has come into the world, and men loved the darkness rather than the Light, for their deeds were evil* (John 3:18, 19).

It is said that a vessel once sighted an enemy at sundown and kept up a cannonade until the darkness put a stop to it. When the sun arose the next morning, they were chagrined to find that the supposed enemy was an immense rock that remained intact after many hours of bombarding. So in all ages, men have been demolishing the Bible as the enemy of the human race, but the Old Book still stands, silent but solid as the Rock of Ages. For trifling skeptics, John 8:21, 24 is very good at showing the consequences of unbelief, while John 5:40 discloses the origin of their skepticism. *You are unwilling to come to Me that you may have life.*

Another class of doubters is really desirous of knowing the truth. As someone has expressed it, "He wishes there was a God to whom he could come as a child to his father. However, he does not know whether there is or not, but he wants to know. He wishes he were an immortal spirit but is not sure that he is anything more than an animated machine, and he seeks for evidence. He would be glad to believe that this unknown God has provided for this unknown soul some way by which it could know both its Father and itself. He does not disbelieve in God or Christ, but he does not know, and he wants to know." For such people, there are two paths to the light, the intellectual and the moral. The first begins with the known and argues its way to the unknown. The creation proves a Creator. Intelligent and moral beings imply a Creator capable of producing such. The *Intelligent and moral beings imply a Creator capable of producing such.* scientific method results only in a high degree of probability, it is true, but then we act every day on such probabilities and ought to act upon them in religion.

The other method starts with the distinction between right and wrong, which we all know and no moral man can doubt. Into this world has come Jesus of Nazareth. He meets our ideals, He commends Himself to our consciences, and He commands our will. If we look at His life and follow His teachings, we will soon find our way into the light. *I am the Light of the world; he who follows Me will not walk in the darkness, but will have the Light of life* (John 8:12). *If anyone is willing to do His will, he will know of the teaching, whether it is of God or whether I speak from Myself* (John 7:17).

Some years ago, a man came to a pastor's study in great perplexity. The pastor asked him to state his problem. First, there was the problem of the triune nature of God, which he could not understand. Neither could he harmonize the foreknowledge of God with the free agency of man. Last of all, he wanted to know if a real dove came down on the head of Jesus when He was baptized. After he unburdened his heart, the pastor told him frankly that he could not explain a single one of these questions but hoped to know sometime. If the man would come to him a hundred years later, he thought he could explain them if the man were still in doubt.

Then he began to ask what these questions had to do with the duty of repentance and faith in Christ, insisting upon a good and sufficient reason for such delay. The man sat lost in thought for a few moments, and then rising, he said with great intensity, "I will arise and go to my Father." He put out his hand to the minister, held it for a moment, and then went quietly on his way. From that decision, he never wavered. He took up the duties of the Christian life at once and soon joined the church. He became a very efficient worker and lived and died a strong Christian. Years after, when his pastor inquired what had become of his doubts, he answered that he had long since forgotten them and affirmed that from that memorable evening when he decided to obey God according to the best light he had, his doubts had never entered his mind.

Dealing with Those Who Doubt the Divinity of Christ

Call attention to the following facts and ask the doubter to read the passages of Scripture carefully and without prejudice.

1. Prophecies relating to Christ were uttered hundreds of years before He was born (Ps. 16:9-11; 22:1, 8, 18; 68:18; Isaiah 7:14; 9:1-6; 40:9-11, 53). These prophecies foretell where Christ should be born, the family of which He should be born, the way in which He should be received (a way entirely different from what would be expected), His death and the precise manner of it, His burial with

all the accompanying circumstances, and His resurrection, ascension, and final victory.

2. The New Testament ascribes to Christ divine titles that the Old Testament applies to God (Heb. 1:8). *But of the Son He says, Your throne, O God, is forever and ever.* In John 20:28, Thomas answered and said to Him, *My Lord and my God*, and Jesus did not rebuke him.

3. In Heb. 1:3, 10, the creation of the world is ascribed to Christ. In Acts 20:28, we have the expression, *The church of God which He purchased with His own blood.* Here, the Holy Spirit describes the blood of Christ as the blood of God Himself.

4. Scriptures teach that Jesus Christ should be worshipped as God. Heb. 1:6, *And let all the angels of God worship Him.* John 5:23, *All will honor the Son even as they honor the Father.* Phil. 2:10-11, *That at the name of Jesus every knee will bow . . . and that every tongue will confess that Jesus Christ is Lord, to the glory of God the Father.*

5. Jesus distinctly claims to be equal with God and entitled to the same honor and adoration. He also assumes divine authority and power. *I and the Father are one* (John 10:30). *He who has seen Me has seen the Father* (John 14:9). When the high priest asked Him at His trial if He were the Christ, the Son of the Blessed One, Jesus answered, *I am; and you shall see* THE SON OF MAN SITTING AT THE RIGHT HAND OF POWER, *and* COMING WITH THE CLOUDS OF HEAVEN (Mark 14:62).

6. In John 5:33, 36, 37, 39, Jesus calls attention to the fourfold witness of John the Baptist, the Father who had borne witness to His Son-ship on several occasions by a voice from heaven, His own mighty miraculous works,

and the Scriptures of the Old Testament which prophesied of Him and in Him found their culmination. In John 9:35-37, Jesus says to the man who had been born blind, *"Do you believe in the Son of God?" He answered, "Who is He, Lord, that I may believe in Him?" Jesus said unto him, "You have both seen Him, and He is the one who is talking with you."*

7. 1 John 2:22, 23 shows that whoever denies the divinity of Jesus is a liar. *Who is the liar but the one who denies that Jesus is the Christ? This is the antichrist, the one who denies the Father and the Son. Whoever denies the Son does not have the Father; the one who confesses the Son has the Father also.*

    1 John 5:12 shows that those who deny the divinity of Christ make God a liar and cannot be saved, for *He who has the Son has life; he who does not have the Son of God does not have life.* In John 8:24, Jesus tells the Pharisees that unless they believe in Him, they shall die in their sins.

8. John 10:33 shows that Jesus Christ was put to death by the Unitarians of His day. *The Jews answered Him, "For a good work we do not stone You, but for blasphemy; and because You, being a man, make Yourself out to be God."*

9. The position that many take that Jesus is simply a good man but not divine is untenable. Either He was what He claimed to be, or else He was the greatest impostor the world has ever seen. That He was not an impostor is demonstrated by two things. First, His resurrection from the dead is the best attested fact in history. Surely, God would not have vindicated the claim of an impostor by raising Him from the dead, receiving Him up into heaven, pouring out the Holy Spirit at Pentecost, and enabling innumerable signs and miracles in the

name of Jesus. Second, that He was not an impostor is shown by the influence that His life and teaching have had upon the world, transforming the lives of millions, making bad men good and good men better, converting drunkards, murderers, and libertines into saints, and leading multitudes out of idolatry and sin into the light and liberty of the Gospel.

10. Some claim that Jesus was thoroughly sincere in all He said but was mistaken and simply imagined Himself to be the Son of God. They refer to what they call the contradictions in His testimony. For instance, in one place, He says, "I and My Father are one," and in another, "The Father is greater than I." They say He cannot be one with God and, at the same time, the Son of God. A young man once raised this objection in the inquiry room, and the preacher replied, "Suppose that you had been on earth when Jesus was here and had heard Him make these contradictory statements. You may have asked Him, 'Master, I do not quite understand you. A little while ago, you said, "He who has seen Me has seen the Father." Now you say, "My Father is greater than I."' And suppose He had said in reply, 'My child, what if, for your redemption from sin, I voluntarily laid aside My eternal glory, and suffered myself to be born of a woman? This would limit My being to the conditions of your nature, that I might, in that nature, offer to God a sacrifice for sin that would enable Him to proclaim forgiveness of sins to the whole world. I am indeed one with the Father, but for the atonement, I have voluntarily assumed an inferior position. Thus, I might take your place and die, which I could not have

> *That Jesus was not an impostor is shown by the influence that His life and teaching have had upon the world.*

done without taking a subordinate place and your very nature. So I sometimes speak of My eternal relation to God and sometimes of My relation to Him as the messenger of the covenant sent forth to redeem."

He listened attentively and then said, "Did Christ ever make such an explanation? He was asked to read Philippians 2:5-8. He read it and said, "Wonderful! Wonderful! Yes, the Son of God made Himself of no reputation for me, took my nature, and died on the cross for me!" Then looking up, he said, "What do I have to do about it?"

"Accept Him, believe on Him, and confess Him as your Savior."

"May I?" Opening his Bible, the preacher turned to Romans 10:9 and read, *That if you confess with your mouth Jesus as Lord, and believe in your heart that God raised Him from the dead, you will be saved.*

"Let me see that!"

He took the book, read it aloud, and then said: "I do believe in my heart that God raised Him from the dead, and I do acknowledge Him as my Savior."

The preacher and the inquirer dropped upon their knees to thank God for this decision and to invoke His aid in remaining a Christian, and thus was the young rationalist converted.

Chapter 17

A Young Man's Difficulties in Coming Out as a Christian

"The fellows I go with don't believe in this sort of thing."

1. Would it not be better for them if they did? And how do you know but that your example might lead them to do some serious thinking? They are likely in the same condition you are—conscious that they ought to be Christians but holding back for fear of what others will say. What those fellows need is a good, healthy jar, something that will show them what cowards they are and the nobility and manliness of following one's convictions.

The Bible says that men are like sheep. One peculiarity of sheep is their lack of independence. They are great imitators; if one goes over the wall, the whole flock goes tumbling after him. You may hold their head or heels, but they will go, taking you with them, unless you let go. It does not matter whether the leader is rushing into safety or peril; the whole flock follows blindly after him.

Young men are much the same. They go in droves; they

think and act as their leader does. If he buys a certain style of hat or neck wear, the others do the same. If one goes to college, half a dozen more may follow.

Now, considering this peculiarity of human nature, why not take advantage of it? Try to lead your associates in the right direction instead of following them in the wrong direction. Why should not you be the Moses who leads them out of Egypt and into the Promised Land? *Who knows whether you have not attained royalty for such a time as this?* (Esther 4:14).

A student at Yale College once went to New Britain, Conn., to take the place of the principal in the high school for a short time. His associate teacher told him it was the custom to open the school with Scripture reading and prayer. Though he was not a Christian, he felt he must comply with the custom and did so. After a few days, he said to his associate, "I feel that I am playing the part of a hypocrite, and I hardly know what to do. My class at Yale holds its class prayer meeting tomorrow night, and I have half a mind to go down and tell them what a predicament I am in and ask them to pray for me." His assistant urged him to go and offered to open the school for him the next morning.

Every man must give an account of himself unto Christ, and your companions' neglect of duty will not justify yours.

He went, told his story in a manly way, and was converted. As a result, a revival sprang up in which eighty students at Yale were led to Christ.

2. Whether your companions follow your example or not, you cannot afford to follow theirs. The issue is too great. You cannot afford to stifle your convictions and jeopardize your soul because they do. Every man must give an account of himself unto Christ, and their neglect of duty will not justify yours. You

need to declare your independence and not be kept from the nobler life and larger liberty of the Gospel by a lot of "fellows."

Strike out for yourself. Let them see that there is one person in that crowd who has the courage of his convictions and is not afraid of what others may say. Do not wander in the wilderness of sin any longer simply because others do. Break loose from them even if you have to do it alone, but perhaps you will not be alone. Tell the fellows in a manly way that you choose to follow Christ and ask them to join you. How do you know but that this is just what they are waiting for?

3. Whether the others follow you or not, they will certainly have more respect for you. A young soldier who had just enlisted found he was the only Christian in his tent. It was not easy to kneel and pray before the others, but he did it. At once, they began to laugh and mock him, and at times, they threw shoes at him. The young man was troubled and did not know what to do. Finally, he went to the regiment chaplain and asked for his advice. The chaplain told him that, under the circumstances, he thought it would be justifiable to say his prayers in silence after he had retired. Meeting him a few days later, the chaplain inquired how he was getting on. "Well, chaplain, I followed your advice for a night or two, but I felt so bad that I could not do it any longer. So I went back to the old way of kneeling by my bedside, and do you know, chaplain, some of the boys have been converted. Now, we have a prayer meeting in the tent every night."

Before you decide on this question, take one good look at "the fellows" and another at Calvary. Ask yourself which has done the most for you and which is most worthy of your love and loyalty. Only One has died for you, only One can forgive your sins, and only One can satisfy every craving of your heart. That One is Jesus Christ, the only leader in this world whom it is perfectly safe to follow. You can worship Him without idolatry and love Him without disappointment. He it is who has said, *He who follows Me will not walk in the darkness, but will have the Light of life* (John 8:12) and *The one who comes to Me I will certainly not cast out* (John 6:37).

If you come out boldly for Christ, you will find that whether "the fellows" follow you or not, you have certainly made it easier for them to do so.

"I did something once which gave me a bad record."

1. Very likely, but remember that all who have ever been saved had made a bad record of some kind. There was Peter. He had good qualities, but he also had certain bad habits which called forth some sharp rebukes from the Master. These doubtless cost Peter many a sleepless night. He was rash and impulsive, always saying the wrong thing. Even after he had been with the Master for three whole years, he was guilty of falsehood and profanity. However, Peter, by the grace of God, overcame his bad record. What is more, he so gained the victory over his besetting sins that his testimony in later life was *protected by the power of God through faith for a salvation ready to be revealed in the last time* (1 Peter 1:5). This swearing, lying fisherman was so transformed by Jesus Christ that he became the corner-stone of the Christian church.

Then there was Mark the backslider, who, not discouraged by his signal failure, made a fresh start and became so steadfast and reliable that the Holy Spirit selected him to write a history of the Master's life. Today, millions of people are prayerfully studying the Gospel of Mark and thanking God for it. Little did he expect such a career when he was trudging home alone after deserting Paul and Barnabas at Pamphylia, but God knows how to use even a backslider to His glory.

Paul, too, had a bad record to contend with. He was even

a persecutor of the church. He dragged women and children through the streets, and no gentleman would do that. He compelled Christians to kneel and blaspheme the name of Jesus, which they loved so dearly. He was cruel, vindictive, and bigoted. Yet, Paul, by the grace of God, became one of the most useful men the world has ever known.

David was a murderer and an adulterer, but today, the whole Christian church is feeding upon his inspired and inspiring words and thanking God that he ever lived. Yes, a bad record is a bad thing, of course, but it does not need to prevent one from being a Christian. It does not need to keep one out of heaven. Indeed, heaven is full of people who once were liars, thieves, murderers, and libertines.

2. Remember that Christ did not come to select a perfect man here and there and thus make up a church. No, He came to seek and to save the lost. He is not looking for righteous men at all but for sinners. He came expressly to lead such to repentance. His encouragement is that He has borne the penalty of their sins on the cross, and whosoever will may be saved. The strange thing about the gospel is that it reveals God's love for those who have made a bad record and His desire to blot it out and give them a chance to make a new record.

Have you ever noticed the great variety of ways in which God describes the putting away of the believer's sins? In Isaiah 38:17, we read, *For You have cast all my sins behind Your back."* "But," someone might say, "God might turn around, and all my sins would be in full sight." Sure enough, and so we read in Micah 7:19, *You will cast all their sins into the depths of the sea."* That is better, but might they wash ashore? Very true, and so God says in Psalm 103:12, *As far as the east is from the west, So far has He removed our transgressions from us."* That is better still, for that means out of God's sight. However, some poor sinner would be sure to say, "Yes, my sins are out of God's sight, but not out of His mind. Every time I meet Him in heaven, I shall feel He is thinking of the terrible things I did on earth." For the sake of such people, God adds another verse, *And their sins and their lawless deeds I will remember no more* (Hebrews 10:17).

Now, why should you so persistently remember what God so graciously forgets? Why should you keep in the foreground what God is willing to put behind His

Why should you
so persistently
remember what God so
graciously forgets?

back? Just throw that bad record in with the rest of your sins and have them all disposed of at once, and then you can have the sweet consciousness that though you may remember your sins, God has entirely forgotten them. Remember also that the longer you wait, the worse your record will be.

3. While your bad record will hinder you somewhat, it will also help you. It will tend to keep you humble for one thing, which will be no small gain. It will enable you to sympathize with others who have made a bad record and to encourage them to hope for better things. Indeed, your bad record, in one sense, will become your strongest weapon of warfare. Why is it that John B. Gough and Francis Murphy were able to lead thousands of drinking men to accept Christ where able and eloquent preachers failed? Because these two men knew by bitter experience all the shame, misery, and hopelessness of a drunkard's life. They also knew by blessed experience that Jesus Christ has the power to break the drunkard's chains and set the captive free. The very thing that hindered and discouraged them before they knew Christ became their most effective weapon after conversion. While David mourned bitterly his great sin in the murder of Uriah, the fifty-first Psalm, which records his grief and penitence, has doubtless led more sinners to repentance

than any chapter in the whole Bible. Thus, God overrules the sins of men and causes *all things to work together for good to those who love God* (Romans 8:28).

4. Consider also that if you have an appalling record, your conversion will be a more incredible triumph of grace than if you were only an ordinary sinner. Jesus Christ claims that He can save the worst of sinners and so change the vilest man or woman on earth by the power of His grace so that He will actually be proud of them in heaven. He is searching the world for difficult cases to demonstrate His power.

If you have a violent temper, a vicious disposition, or a depraved appetite, you are just the kind of a subject that the Master is looking for. He can use you to a far better advantage for some purposes than if you were a nice young man who had been sheltered from temptation all your life. If you will let Him take control of your life and change it by His grace, He can convince hundreds of other sinners that He is just the Savior they need. Here is a great opportunity to serve your day and generation and glorify Christ. That very record of which you are so ashamed is the very thing which will enable you to do it.

5. Could it be that in heaven those who have been the greatest sinners will be the loudest praisers of the Redeemer's name? When the Pharisee criticized Jesus for allowing the outcast woman to weep at His feet, the Master said, *"Simon, I have something to say to you. . . . A moneylender had two debtors: one owed five hundred denarii, and the other fifty. When they were unable to repay, he graciously forgave them both. So which of them will love him more?" Simon answered and said, "I suppose the one whom he forgave more." And He said to him, "You have judged correctly."* (Luke 7:40-43). He then drew a contrast between the proud, self-righteous host and the sinful, sorrowing

woman who was weeping out her penitence and bathing His feet with her tears. Even so, our theme in heaven will not be the good deeds we have wrought on earth but the matchless grace that redeemed us, and the greater the sins from which we have been redeemed, the greater triumph of grace we shall have to proclaim.

Chapter 18

Common Objections and How to Deal With Them

"I Have No Time for Religion"

When a man offers this excuse, it means that he is not interested. He has all the time there is, and if he considered his salvation a matter of much importance, he would take time for it. He may be so crowded with business and home that he cannot attend many meetings, but that need not prevent him from being a Christian. Our Roman Catholic acquaintances, who belong almost wholly to the laboring class and whose time is not their own, as a rule, are the most regular churchgoers in the community. The fact is that people find time for what they consider important.

I know a young man who wished to attend a certain series of meetings. The factory where he was employed was running evenings. Every man was expected to work overtime for a few weeks during the busy season, for which, of course, they received extra pay. He was not a Christian but went to his employer and asked to be excused from working evenings for a week. He also went without supper each night to attend the services. Very soon, he gave his heart to God; and before the end of the week, he had the pleasure of seeing his brother converted through his instrumentality.

When one offers the lack of time as an excuse for not being a Christian, it is well to show him by some simple illustration that this is not the real reason. Say to him,

"If, in addition to your regular work, you had an opportunity to earn one hundred dollars each week by one hour of extra work, would you accept the offer?"

He will doubtless answer, "I think I would."

"In other words, if you want time for something extra, you manage to find it. You see, my friend, the simple fact is that you do not feel the need for salvation and are not interested in it. You are in the condition described in Ephesians 4:18, *Being darkened in their understanding, excluded from the life of God because of the ignorance that is in them, because of the hardness of their heart.* Why not face the fact, disagreeable as it may be? When people ask you why you are not a Christian, give them the real reason instead of offering a false one. Furthermore, if you do not take time to consider this question of salvation, you will soon lose your capacity to know God and will be in the condition described in the nineteenth verse of the same chapter, *they, having become callous, have given themselves over to sensuality for the practice of every kind of impurity with greediness.*

> *Repentance towards God and love to one's fellow men does not conflict with anyone's duty.*

Remind him that religion does not consist of sermons and prayer meetings but of maintaining a certain attitude towards God, which he can assume in a moment and maintain in the midst of the busiest life. Repentance towards God and love to one's fellow men does not conflict with anyone's duty, nor is it a waste of time. On the contrary, it saves time, sweetens toil, and enriches the whole life.

"I Will Think about It"

Some minds mature very slowly, and if one really has never considered what is involved in becoming a Christian, it may be well to give him a little time for reflection.

As a rule, however, this excuse is only another way of saying, "Not now." We should show the person that he already has all the information he needs for an intelligent decision. If he waited a dozen years, he would not be any better prepared, but on the contrary, he would be less disposed to decide than now.

There are only two things that he needs to know: he is lost, and Christ is the only Savior. These two things he knows already, and all that remains for him to do is to accept Christ as his Savior. Show him that continual thinking on the subject will not make the decision any easier, but continual rejection of Christ will surely make it harder. An old man in New Britain, Conn., publicly confessed Christ one night. When asked if this was the first time he seriously considered the matter, he replied, "No, I have been thinking hard on this question for over thirty years." One moment of decision accomplished more for him than thirty years of thinking.

It is a great mistake for people to think that they can be saved when they please. The only time a man can be saved is when God chooses to save him, and God's time is now. *Behold, now is "the acceptable time," behold, now is "the day of salvation"* (2 Cor. 6:2).

No one has a right to say that he will think it over and decide when he is ready. God calls for an immediate decision. He commands us to lay down the weapons of our rebellion and surrender unconditionally.

When Mr. Moody was holding meetings in Hartford, Conn., many years ago, he urged a man to accept Christ at once one night. Finally, the man replied, "Well, Mr. Moody, I will promise you this. I will attend the meeting tomorrow night and accept Christ as my Savior then." That man never reached his home alive. The train on which he traveled ran off a bridge at Tariffville, and many lost their lives. Among them was the man who promised Mr. Moody that he would repent the next night. "That experience," said Mr. Moody, "taught me a lesson: never to let anyone off with a promise, but to press them hard for an immediate decision, and if that failed, to show them the peril of even a night's delay."

Tomorrow is the devil's time. Do not trust him. He is a deceiver and the father of lies from the beginning.

"So Many Conflicting Opinions"

Occasionally, we meet a person who claims there are so many conflicting opinions among Christians that he does not know what to believe. Remind him that the differences of opinion, as a rule, relate to minor matters, such as the mode of baptism or the method of church government, and not to the vital question of salvation.

All evangelical denominations agree that there is only one way of salvation from sin: repentance towards God and faith in the Lord Jesus Christ.

While they may differ some as to forms of worship and methods of government, it is foolish for one to divert his attention to these side issues and lose sight of the main question. Besides, it is an indication of mental laziness when one is not willing to search the Scriptures and form an opinion of his own. God has given us the Bible, which reveals His will, and a mind capable of understanding it (John 20:31). God's will concerning the way of salvation is revealed so clearly that even a child can understand it. What excuse have we then for deferring our duty?

We have no right to hold this matter of repentance in suspense simply because there are some things in the Bible that we do not understand. There will always be things we do not understand, and if we wait until we understand everything, we shall never be saved. If we will obey that part of God's Word that we do understand, we will soon get light on some of the obscure things.

Daniel Webster states his position very clearly in a letter written to a friend: "I believe that God exists in three persons; this I learn from revelation alone. Nor is it any objection to this belief that I cannot comprehend how one can be three or three one. I hold it my duty to believe not what I can comprehend or account for but what my Maker teaches me. I believe religion to be a matter not of demonstration but of faith. God requires us to give credit to the truths He reveals, not because we can prove them, but because He reveals them."

> *If we wait until we understand everything, we shall never be saved.*

At one time, there was a great revival at Yale College. Horace Bushnell was the most popular tutor in college, but he was not a Christian. He knew that his position was a stumbling block to some of the students, and it troubled him greatly. He said to himself, "I don't believe in the Bible, and I do not believe that Jesus Christ is the Son of God. I cannot play the part of a hypocrite just to help others. What can I do?" A voice seemed to say to him,

"Horace Bushnell, what do you believe anyhow?"

"Well, one thing I believe is that there is an absolute difference between right and wrong."

"Well, have you ever taken a stand on what you do believe? Have you ever taken your stand on the right to follow it wherever it carries you, even if it carries you over the Niagara Falls?"

"No, I never have, but I will."

He prayed, "O God, if there is any God, show me if Jesus Christ is your Son, and if you will show me that, I promise to accept Him as my Savior and confess Him before the world."

In a short time, the light burst upon his soul. Horace Bushnell came out on the side of Christ, and almost every young man at Yale was converted.

I once met a man on the train who claimed to be a skeptic. He said there were so many different religions that he did not know what to believe. "One claims that we ought to worship Buddha and another Confucius. Some say that Mormonism is the true religion, and I suppose you would say that Jesus Christ was the only Savior. In the midst of all these conflicting opinions, how is one to know what to believe?"

I said to him, "My friend, did you ever embrace any one of these religions?"

"No, sir."

"You remember the fable about the horse which stood between two stacks of hay. He was about to take a bite from one when a smell of clover came from the other so inviting that he hesitated. Then he caught a whiff from the other that led him to turn again. Finally, he starved to death between the two stacks because he could not decide between them.

"Now, my friend, are you not making the same mistake the horse made? Here you stand in the midst of all these religions, starving your soul because you do not know which one to choose. Had you not better embrace one of them and do it quickly? If you think that Buddhism is the most promising, become a Buddhist. If you think Mormonism is from God, become a Mormon. If you find salvation from sin in these religions, continue in them, but if not, then accept Christ as your Savior, and I am sure you will find salvation in Him. He is the true, 'seek no further.' But, by all means, embrace some religion, and do it quickly, for you are starving your soul for the lack of Some One to worship and obey."

"I believe there is some truth in what you say," said the man, "but this is my station, and I must leave you. I am glad we have had this conversation, and I hope we shall meet again."

Apparently, the man was convinced of his mistake and was becoming interested, but he was leaving the car, and what could I do? I thought of the little package of leaflets which I usually carry, and selecting a couple, I rushed out on the platform and gave them to him. One was the Christian Life Card, and the other was a leaflet written by Dr. J. W. Chickering of Washington, D.C. Before he died, the author had the names of over seventeen hundred people who had either written or told him personally that they attributed their conversions to this tract.

Then I commended the man to God, hoping that the next Christian who met him might lead him further along. Perhaps some of my readers have met him. What success did you have?

Chapter 19

Backsliders and How to Deal with Them

Backsliders may be divided into three classes.

1. Those who have never been converted but have once considered themselves Christians. The churches are full of people who, at some time, received a religious impulse and perhaps expressed their purpose to lead a Christian life but never really received Christ.

Such people must be shown in a kind and loving way that they have been mistaken, or they will never be willing to make another trial. It is well to point out some of the evidences of the new birth and let them see that they have never experienced it.

Romans 8:1 shows that the Christian is delivered from the guilt of sin. Ask them if they have ever been wholly free from a sense of guilt and for what reason. 1 John 3:14 proves that we have passed from death unto life because we love the brethren. 1 John 3:21, 22 shows that an obedient Christian will have answers to prayer. 1 John 4:13 ensures the fellowship of the Holy Spirit. Test a person with such passages, and he will soon recognize his true position.

At the close of a service, I was introduced to a young man who said, "I have tried this thing two or three times, and it did not seem to work, and I do not care to try it again." He spoke of conversion as if it were something like vaccination, which did not "take" in his case.

"Were you ever really converted?"

"I do not know."

"Did you ever get a new heart?"

"I doubt if I did."

"You have been trying to live the Christian life without Christ to help you, haven't you?"

"That describes it."

"It is no wonder you have had a hard time. It is like trying to run a watch without a mainspring. You might shake it, and the wheels would run a minute or two, but it would soon stop. It is also impossible to lead a Christian life without the help of Christ, who is the mainspring of it all.

"If you had the very Christ who gave the commandments in your heart to help you, would you not be able to keep them?"

"I think I would."

"Listen then," I said, and I quoted Ezekiel 36:26-27. *I will give you a new heart and put a new spirit within you; and I will remove the heart of stone from your flesh and give you a heart of flesh. I will put My Spirit within you and cause you to walk in My statutes, and you will be careful to observe My ordinances.*

"This is God's offer to you, a new heart. Will you accept it?" In a moment or two, he was on his knees, asking God for a new heart.

2. The second class consists of those who have drifted away from God by disobedience and are not anxious to return. They are like the prodigal before his money was spent. They are living

worldly lives, and as long as health and prosperity continue, they get along fairly well without God. However, they have many rebukes of conscience and frequent longings for the good old days of fellowship with God.

With such people, Jeremiah 2:5 is a good verse. Ask them what fault they could find with God that caused them to wander from Him. Jeremiah 2:13 is also good. Ask them if it is not true that their present life is evil and bitter compared to the fellowship and joy God provides for those who obey Him. Show them the ingratitude and sin of such a course. Quote Jeremiah 2:19 and show them the folly of turning from a fountain of pure water to a broken cistern or a muddy pool. Then ask them if the self-life is not a broken cistern compared to that well of water that Christ opens in every heart that receives Him.

3. Backsliders who are tired of sin and anxious to return to God. They are like the prodigal after his money is spent and after months of hunger and loneliness in the far country. For such, Hosea 14:1, 4 is a good passage. *Return, O Israel, to the* LORD *your God, For you have stumbled because of your iniquity. . . . I will heal their apostasy, I will love them freely, For My anger has turned away from them."*

> *The backslider is despised by the world, a reproach to the church, and alienated from God, and he condemns himself.*

The most effective passage, however, is Luke 15:11-24. This not only pictures the wretched condition of the backslider, but it shows the steps by which he must return and the royal reception that awaits him. No one needs pity more than the backslider. He is despised by the world, a reproach to the church, and alienated from God, and he condemns himself.

We should sympathize with backsliders all the more because, at some time or other, we have all belonged to that class ourselves.

We know by sad experience how bitter it is to miss the sunshine of God's favor and to walk in the darkness of His displeasure.

How thankful should we be that God has laid bare His heart and given us in Luke 15 such a beautiful picture of His secret longing and watching for the prodigal's return and His hearty and abundant forgiveness of all past offenses the moment we repent of them.

Chapter 20

The Appeal to Students

M r. Gladstone was once asked what the leading question in England was at that time. He replied that there was but one leading question at that time, or at any time, and that was the question of one's relation to the Lord Jesus Christ. He then went on to say that the most intelligent men were those who paid the most attention to this subject. "I have known personally all the men who have been prominent in England during the last fifty years, in business, politics, or literature, and of the sixty most prominent men, fifty-four have been professing Christians."

If Mr. Gladstone was right and one's relation to Christ is the leading question that confronts a student, he must settle it early. Indeed, this question lies at the basis of all education. What is the real object of education? It is to increase one's capacity to know God and to make Him known to others. This is what education is for, what life is for. *This is eternal life, that they may know You, the only true God, and Jesus Christ whom You have sent* (John 17:3).

1. The keenest delight of which we are capable comes to us from knowing God. When the devout astronomer Kepler made his great discovery, he exclaimed, "O God, I think Thy thoughts after Thee." There is no greater joy than this unless it is seeing God's character reproduced in our lives. If this is true, then education is not optional but imperative. We are bound to cultivate every talent we possess because each is an avenue through which God can reveal Himself to us. We are bound to open every window of our soul "towards Jerusalem" and let in the light of God's glorious truth.

   No wonder the Great Teacher said, *Take My yoke upon you and learn from Me . . . . and you will find rest for your souls* (Matthew 11:29). Young people have souls as well as minds, and the one needs training quite as much as the other. It is possible to develop the mind at the expense of the soul and to leave the spiritual nature in a dwarfed and stunted condition. Indeed, is it not possible for a student to go forth with a well-trained mind and irreproachable morals and still fall far short of being a whole man because he does not know God? *Having no hope, and without God in the world* (Eph. 2:12). The Greek student does not need to be told that "without God" means "atheist."

2. The superior advantages students enjoy make it doubly important that they become acquainted early with the Lord Jesus. Education enlarges one's capacity to see, foresee, do, and undo. It multiplies his influence and thus increases his responsibility since the welfare of others depends upon his action and attitude. No educated person can

possibly live a Christless life without leading others to do the same. This consideration should have great weight. A professor in a large military school recently told the writer that it was the thought of his influence with the boys that led him to decide for God and put himself on record as a Christian.

3. Again, the peculiar temptations that confront a student make an acquaintance with Jesus indispensable. Among these may be mentioned:

   a. The freedom from home restraint. The strong, steadying hand of the father and the indescribable influence of the mother is lacking. There is no younger brother or sister to be considered, not even the restraining influence of someone else's sister. The consequence is that one grows selfish and thinks that all the world was made for him.

   b. The petty vices which prevail so commonly among students. By the side of the writer in college sat the valedictorian of the class. He was a well-disposed man, but he had no religious principles. When others drank, he was not strong enough to refuse. After graduation, he studied law and became one of the most brilliant and promising lawyers in the state. Temptations now grew stronger and more frequent. Having no acquaintance with him *able also to save forever* (Heb. 7:25) and *able to keep you from stumbling* (Jude 24), he soon lost his standing and business and died a common drunkard.

   c. Not the least of the dangers that confront a student is the temptation to doubt. He lives in an atmosphere of inquiry and criticism. Old theories are being laid aside, and new facts are constantly being discovered. Possibly, he sees some of his instructors, for whose ability he has the highest respect, utterly indifferent to the claims of the Gospel. Literature is full of covert sneers at religion. He is just at the age when his critical faculties are being developed, and he begins to question everything that he once believed. Add to this the natural willingness of the heart to have it so, and you have a combination of circumstances calculated to shake the strongest faith. Some indeed think it a sign of superior intellect to doubt, but this is a mistake. It is sometimes a sign of spiritual blindness and often of moral obliquity. A large part of the skepticism of students is of the heart rather than of the head.

4. Without Christ, you can never have a satisfactory philosophy of life. "Where did I come from? Why am I here? Where am I going?" These are questions that will forever remain answerable. Life will be an enigma, and doubts will darken your dying hour. Become acquainted with Christ, and doubts begin to disappear. You see what kind of a man you really are, and in the person of Christ, you see what you ought to be. You also discover how this change is to be wrought: through Christ's death for you on the cross, and the reproduction of His life in you by the Holy Spirit. This is no dream or fiction but a blessed reality, and he who commits the keeping of his life to the Lord Jesus will soon find it so.

5. Without Christ, you can never do your best work. You have insatiable cravings that no one can satisfy but the Lord Jesus. You have a fund of energy that no one can control, doubts that no one can dispel, and powers of usefulness that no one can develop so well as the Savior. Jesus Christ is as indispensable to a thinking man as sunshine to a flower.

Consider, too, the inconsistency of searching all creation for facts and yet ignoring the greatest fact in the world's history: Christ died and rose again. This alone, the best-attested fact in history, makes the appeal to become a Christian supremely rational. If you refuse the appeal, it devolves on you to give the reason why.

6. One's capacity to know God weakens by disuse and may be utterly lost. Charles Darwin said in his early life, "I believe God will reveal Himself to every individual soul, and my most passionate desire is a deeper and clearer vision of God. But one can easily lose all belief in the spiritual by giving up the continual thought and care for spiritual things." Near the end of his life, he said, "In my younger days, I was deeply religious, but I made my mind a kind of machine for grinding out general laws in the material world, and my spiritual nature atrophied." His last days were clouded with sadness and spiritual gloom.

Christ died and rose again. This alone makes the appeal to become a Christian supremely rational.

J. Douglas Adam, of New York, said at a Northfield Conference a few years ago, "A friend of mine was once on a parliamentary commission with Prof. T. H. Huxley. They happened to stay at a little country inn over Sunday. Huxley said to my friend, 'I suppose you are going to church this morning?'

"'I am; I always go to church.'

"'I know you do,' said Huxley, 'but suppose this morning you sit down and talk with me about religion – simple experimental religion.'

"'I will,' said my friend, 'if you mean it.'

"They sat down together, and my friend, out of a deep and rich experience, told him of the cross of Christ and pardoning love. After three hours, Huxley's eyes filled with tears, and he put out his hand and said, 'If I could only believe that, I would be willing to give my right hand.' What do you call that but intellectual bondage? Huxley was perhaps the greatest scientific enemy of Christianity in our generation.

"The same friend told me that again and again Mr. John Morley would come to him in the lobby of the House of Commons and put his hand in his and say, 'I want you to pray for me. I am going to Ireland on important executive business, and I want your prayers.' But now, Morley is perhaps the leading literary agnostic today."

What a pitiful picture! Two masterful minds so imprisoned by reason that they could not believe! Conscious of their need of God, and yet not knowing how to approach Him! A dying man once said to the writer, "I know I ought to turn to God, but I have had my own way so long that now I lack the power to turn. I have lost control of my own will, and I must die as I have lived."

The conclusion is this: every student should accept Christ and do it now. If he waits five years, the chances are that he will never do it. Every year that he puts it off, he loses something of his capacity to discern spiritual truth and to feel its force.

Besides, every day that he puts it off, he loses something he can never regain and God Himself cannot recover for him. He loses part of his possible destiny, part of that great inheritance of character and influence which God has provided for him in Christ Jesus, but which he can lose as surely by simple neglect as by a life of vice or crime.

Every man wishes to make the most of himself. The only possible way to do this is to decide now, for every moment some part of his inheritance is slipping away, never to be regained. Strictly speaking, it is NOW or NEVER.

> *Behold, now is "the acceptable time," behold, now is "the day of salvation"* (2 Cor. 6:2)

Chapter 21

What It Costs Not to Be a Christian

People sometimes refuse Christ because of the sacrifice involved. It costs too much, and they are not willing to pay the price. Yes, it does cost something to be a Christian, but it costs far more not to be a Christian. Let us see what it costs to live and die without Christ.

1. Not being a Christian costs the sacrifice of peace. *Those who love Your law have great peace* (Psalm 119:165). *The steadfast of mind You will keep in perfect peace, Because he trusts in You* (Isaiah 26:3).

This is the portion of the Christian. He has peace with God, the peace of God, and the God of peace besides. The Christless soul knows nothing of this, for *"There is no peace," says my God, "for the wicked"* (Isaiah 57:21).

He knows that he is disobeying God, and he is fearful all

the time. *Who through fear of death were subject to slavery all their lives* (Hebrews 2:15).

Besides, he is conscious of an unseen force that is continually working against him. *The way of the treacherous is hard* (Proverbs 13:15). God makes it hard so that the sinner may weary of it and turn his feet into the path of righteousness. *Therefore, behold, I will hedge up her way with thorns, And I will build a wall against her* (Hosea 2:6).

As surely as all things work together for good to them that love God, so surely does God work against the sinner. The same love that prompts Him to send blessings to the righteous leads Him to send hindrances and warnings to the sinner. The sinner calls it bad luck, but he suspects that it is something more, even the deliberate purpose of God.

> The same love that prompts God to send blessings to the righteous leads Him to send hindrances to the sinner.

A father once said to his son, who was determined to obtain more liquor, "My son, if you go out of this house tonight, you will have to go over the dead body of your father." Even so, the lost sinner has to fight his way down to hell, resisted at every step by his Heavenly Father, and finally tramples underfoot the Son of God. Can there be any peace in such a life?

2. Not being a Christian costs the sacrifice of the highest joy. I do not say that the Christless man will have no joy. He may know the joy of health, friendship, and domestic life and acquire money, power, and fame. But there are nobler joys than these which he loses. He cannot know the joy of sin forgiven, the comfort and companionship of the Holy Spirit, or the joy of becoming like Jesus Christ.

It is God's purpose that all His children shall be joyful, full of joy. *These things I have spoken to you so that My joy may be in you, and that your joy may be made full* (John 15:11). How different the feeling of a Christless soul! A visitor who was calling on the great Bismarck expressed the hope that he might live many days. Bismarck replied, "There is only one happy day left for me. It is the one on which I shall not wake up again."

"Aged friend, how is it that an old man can be so merry and cheerful?" asked one man of another.

"Because I belong to the Lord."

"Are no others happy at your time of life?"

"No, not one." Then straightening up, with the glow of hope upon his countenance, he said, "Listen, please, to the truth from one who knows. Then tell it everywhere, and no man of threescore and ten can be found to gainsay it – the devil has no happy old men."

3. Not being a Christian costs the sacrifice of the highest success in life. Everyone wishes to make the most of himself, but this is impossible unless he yields his life to Christ. God has a plan for every life, and this plan alone assures the highest success. Does not God know what is good for the creature better than the creature himself? It is folly to think that one can live in God's world and achieve success yet disobey the laws of God.

Remember that money, popularity, and power do not constitute success. One may have all these and yet be a consummate failure. The true object of life is to know and do God's will, and the Christless soul misses that completely.

4. Not being a Christian costs the loss of one's soul. Man was made to know God, enjoy Him, and become like Him. This capacity, however, weakens by disuse and may be utterly lost. Charles Lamb claimed that Samuel Taylor Coleridge was the brightest mind that England ever produced. A more modern biographer calls him "an archangel slightly damaged." How

much his character had deteriorated by holding the truth in suspense may be judged by an inscription he wrote at the age of thirty-five on the fly leaf of a Bible his mother had given him.

> "When I received this volume small
> My years were scarcely seventeen;
> When it was hoped I might be all
> Which, then, alas, I might have been.

> "And now my years are thirty-five;
> And every mother hopes her lamb,
> And every other child alive
> May never be, what now I am."

Sin is doing what one wants rather than what he ought to do. *All of us like sheep have gone astray, Each of us has turned to his own way; But the* LORD *has caused the iniquity of us all to fall on Him* (Isaiah 53:6).

This habit of having his own way grows upon the sinner until even God is unable to change it. Neither entreaties, warnings, nor threats can subdue his stubborn will. Indifference to God is followed by disobedience and defiance, and sometimes, the soul curses God to His face.

Not only does the capacity to know God and enjoy Him weaken by disuse, but sin eats out every trace of the divine image until there is nothing left but "the mark of the beast," nothing but the spirit of Satan to whom the sinner has yielded his life, instead of unto God. When all trace of the divine image is gone, there is nothing left for God to love; all He can do is cast it out.

Some time ago, a jeweler in New York had a very hard diamond to polish. Usually, the stones are placed on a wheel under a pressure of two or three pounds. This stone was put under a pressure of forty pounds. The wheel was speeded up to twenty-eight thousand revolutions a minute, and the stone was kept on the wheel for a hundred days. At the end of that time, no impression had been made upon the stone; all that had been accomplished was to throw the jeweler into nervous prostration. The revolutions of that wheel were equal to three times around the globe. The jeweler gave up the job in despair and sent it to the Historical Society as a specimen of a diamond too hard to be polished. Even so, God keeps this world spinning around on its axis not a hundred days but seventy long years in a vain attempt to conform some souls to His image. Finally, sick at heart, he is compelled to cast them away, saying, *Ephraim is joined to idols; Let him alone* (Hosea 4:17).

5. Not being a Christian costs the loss of heaven. The penalty of having one's own way here is to be consigned hereafter to a place where everyone has his own way, which is hell. Perhaps that is at least partially what makes it hell. Heaven is a place where no one has his own way, but all delight to do God's will. That is what makes it heaven. The Christless soul has no hope of heaven; even if he had, he could not enjoy it. Heaven would be hell to one who is not heavenly-minded, to one who does not love Jesus, and who does love sin.

Heaven would be hell to one who does not love Jesus, and who does love sin.

The Christless soul must prepare to part forever from all his dear ones who have chosen Christ: his mother who taught him to pray, his faithful wife, his children whose little hands have long been beckoning to woo him home to heaven. When Dwight L. Moody died, he looked up and said, "Is this death? If so, it is glorious. Earth is receding; heaven is opening. God is calling me." Instead of this welcome, the Christless soul will hear the sad words, "Depart from Me."

Yes, it does cost something to be a Christian. It may cost

you the sacrifice of some pleasure, companions, or money, but not being a Christian will cost you the loss of peace, joy, and real success. It will cost you the loss of your soul. It will cost you heaven. Are you prepared to pay the price?

> *For what will it profit a man if he gains the whole world and forfeits his soul?* (Matt. 16:26).

Chapter 22

Mistakes in Teaching

I t is doubtful if we fully appreciate the importance of the work entrusted to us. Too often, a teacher takes a class because he is urged to do so or because no one else will serve rather than because it is a magnificent opportunity he cannot afford to lose. As a matter of fact, no higher honor can be conferred upon any one than to entrust to him the care of souls.

When the child of Zacharias and Elizabeth was brought into the temple to be circumcised, the relatives and friends who knew the peculiar circumstances attending his birth, the dumbness of his father, and the sudden loosing of his tongue marveled among themselves, saying, "What manner of child shall this be?"

Something of the same mystery and uncertainty attends the birth of every child. Each one is an entirely new combination. In its veins runs the blood of good people and bad, priests and pirates, saints and sinners. Every child has in it the making of an angel or a demon. What it shall be depends not only on what it is but also on how it is taught and trained. If a child from a Christian home were brought up in a heathen family, it would probably become a heathen, and a heathen child under Christian training would probably become a Christian.

How important it is then that we recognize the possibilities of good and evil in every child and that we encourage the good tendencies and suppress the evil. Does not the bloodline affect the formation of character? Certainly. How then can we hope to develop a good character out of a child whose parentage is low and possibly even vicious?

In every child, there runs the blood of many generations. Go far enough back, and a pious and godly ancestry will be found for every child. From these, it inherits a predisposition to righteousness, which will surely affect its character. In Exodus 20:5, we read that God visits *the iniquity of the fathers on the children, on the third and the fourth generations of those who hate Me.* In Deuteronomy 7:9, we read that God *keeps His covenant and His lovingkindness to a thousandth generation with those who love Him and keep His commandments.* In other words, under God's economy, the influence of righteous people is more enduring and permanent than that of the ungodly.

Sin abounds, it is true, but grace much more abounds.

We should never forget that every child has two fathers, an earthly and a Heavenly Father. While on the human side, he may inherit a legacy of evil tendencies, on the divine side, he has in Jesus Christ a legacy of grace that more than counterbalances the evil. Yes, blood does count, but the blood of Jesus Christ counts more than all other influences combined. Sin abounds, it is true, but grace much more abounds. Hence, it follows that as we sometimes find a lily growing in a swamp, so we often find a beautiful character whose immediate ancestors have been even disreputable. It was this, I suppose, to which Paul referred when he said, *Therefore from now on we recognize no one according to the flesh* (2 Cor. 5:16).

It is said that a traveler once called at a house in South Africa and inquired for the head of the family. Some children were playing in the yard, tossing stones from one to another in place of a ball. While waiting for the father, the visitor joined the children in their play. Soon, a stone, which looked like a huge crystal, was tossed into his hand. His experienced eye at once recognized in that rough-looking stone a diamond of enormous size and value. Thus were the diamond mines of South Africa discovered.

Even so, Jesus Christ, a traveler from a far country, first discovered the worth of a human soul. By His testimony concerning them, His tender love for them, and the infinite price He paid for their redemption, He has raised their value throughout the entire world.

He who is wise wins souls, says Solomon (Prov. 11:30), while James adds, *He who turns a sinner from the error of his way shall save his soul from death and shall cover a multitude of sins* (James 5:20). Add to this the purchase price which has been paid for every soul, *shepherd the church of God which He purchased with His own blood* (Acts 20:28).

If you are burdened with a consciousness of your unfitness for the care of souls, remember what someone has truly said. Just as nurses who have the care of a king's children are more generously fed and tenderly cared for than they otherwise would be, so we, to whom the King of kings has entrusted the care of His precious children, may hope to be fed more bountifully with the bread of life and taught more tenderly by the Holy Spirit because of our great responsibility.

A common mistake of teachers is that they do not sufficiently appreciate the forces of evil that are arrayed against us. *For our struggle is not against flesh and blood, but against the rulers, against the powers, against the world forces of this darkness, against the spiritual forces of wickedness in the heavenly places* (Eph. 6:12). The careless and prayerless way in which some teachers prepare for their work shows that they have no adequate idea of the opposition which everyone must encounter who preaches or teaches the gospel. As a matter of fact, every Sunday is a scene of conflict when all the forces of heaven and hell are arrayed against each other. Every Sunday School service is a battlefield on which are decided eternal issues, and the destiny of multitudes is determined. If athletes train for a boat race or ball game, surely the teacher ought to train all week so that he may be in superb spiritual condition on the Lord's Day and have an adequate knowledge of the lesson. He cannot pray too much nor ponder too often the relation of each pupil to Christ and the wisest application to be made of each lesson.

> Every Sunday is a scene of conflict when all the forces of heaven and hell are arrayed against each other.

One of the greatest mistakes many teachers make is not talking frankly with their pupils about their relation to Jesus Christ. They may take great interest in the class and work hard on the lessons, but if they do not have the courage to talk with their pupils personally on the subject of religion, they will never succeed as teachers. Pupils are quick to recognize moral cowardice, and they are sure to despise it.

One of the most successful Sunday School workers that this country has ever produced was Mr. Wm. Reynolds. He was converted from a general worker into a personal worker by the following experience. His pastor was to exchange pulpits on Sunday, and he offered to entertain the visiting minister. When the latter arrived on Saturday night, he met him at the door and gave him a hearty welcome. The visitor was a little man, but he made a great change in that household. Hardly had he removed his hat and coat before he turned to his host and asked,

"What are you doing for God?"

"I am teaching a class in Sunday School."

"Girls or boys?"

"They are young ladies."

"Have they all been converted?"

"I don't know whether they have been converted or not."

"Let us pray," said the visitor, and down he went on his knees right there in the hall, and he prayed fervently for that teacher and his class.

Soon, Mr. Reynolds went to his wife and said, "I don't think much of that man whom we have to entertain over Sunday."

"Why not?"

"Why," said the indignant host, "that fellow got me down on my knees out in the hall and prayed for me because I told him that I didn't know whether my class was converted or not."

"But husband, don't you think the man was more than half right?"

"I thought," said Mr. Reynolds, "it was rather hard for my wife to turn against me, but I tried to make the best of it. Fortunately, we had guests at dinner, and by careful steering, I managed to keep the conversation from running into the subject of religion. After the guests had retired, I pushed the Bible across the table towards the minister and asked him to lead our devotions. (There are some Christian homes where they always have family worship – when a minister is visiting them.) The little minister read a chapter and then, turning to me, said, 'Brother Reynolds, do you have the faith to believe that all your class will be converted tomorrow?'

"I cannot say that I have."

"Then I don't see but one thing to pray for," and down he

went on his knees and prayed that I might have faith given me to lead all my class to Christ the next day. Then he went to bed, and I was glad of it.

After a while, I retired myself, but not to sleep. Somehow, I could not help thinking of my class. There was Mary, a fine girl, capable and earnest. She would make a splendid worker if she were only a Christian, but I am afraid she is not. Then there is Susie. She has many splendid qualities, but I doubt she loves the Savior. Thus, I went over the whole class in my thoughts and finally began to pray for them. The more I prayed, the more anxious I became. Finally, I arose and knelt by the bedside and prayed long and earnestly for my girls. At length, the burden became so intolerable that I went upstairs and woke the little minister, saying, "See here, my friend, you have got me into trouble, and you must help me out of it. I want you to get up and help me pray for my girls."

Out he jumped and joined me in earnest prayer for those seven unsaved girls. The next day, I went to my class and began the lesson. Somehow, I couldn't feel any interest in it, and finally, I threw the lesson aside and said, "Girls, I have a confession to make. I have taught this class for several years. I have worked hard to make the lessons interesting, but I am afraid I haven't been faithful to your souls. I do not even know whether you are Christians or not. How is it with you, Mary? Are you a Christian?"

"No, Mr. Reynolds, I am not, but I would like to be a Christian."

"How is it with you, Susie?"

"I think I am just about where Mary stands. I am not a Christian, but I want to be one."

"And Jenny, how is it with you?"

"I am not a Christian either, but I have long wished I was. I have often wondered why it was, Mr. Reynolds, that you never spoke to us on this subject. You are so interested in us and all that pertains to our welfare, yet you never speak to us about our relation to Christ."

I went through the class, and I found every one of them in the same condition. I said, "Girls, this is no place for us. Follow me into the ladies' parlor." They did so, and all seven girls knelt with me and accepted Christ as their Savior. As soon as I reached home, the little minister greeted me with the question,

"How about those girls, Brother Reynolds?"

"Every one of them was converted this morning."

"Praise the Lord."

"I did praise the Lord, but it made my heart ache to think that I might just as well have had that joy several years before if I had not been such a moral coward."

That was the beginning of a new life for Mr. Reynolds, and thousands of teachers and scholars have had occasion to thank God for him and his helpful words.

If every Sunday School teacher in our land would have a plain talk with his class next Sunday, I believe that thousands, yes hundreds of thousands, of pupils would be converted before the session closed. Will you be one to do it?

Chapter 23

Bible Training Classes

One of the signs of the times is the increasing demand for skilled labor. If a man wishes help, which is worth low wages, he can go out on a street corner in any city and hire a hundred men in about as many minutes. If, however, he wants to hire a professional tradesman, he may have to search for three or four months to find that man. Cheap labor is plenty, but skilled labor is scarce. Manufacturers say that it is very difficult to find men who can take an idea and build a machine to execute it.

Hence, all over the country, technical schools are springing up for training the eye, hand, and voice. There are schools for nurses, journalists, and designers. The world is weary of incompetent help. "Wages are no consideration," they say; "only give us men and women who know how."

The consequence is that it is becoming more and more difficult for untrained laborers to find employment. The time was when anyone could teach school if he happened to have an uncle on the school board, but now it is impossible to secure a good situation unless one has had special instruction in the art of leaching. Twenty-five years ago, every boy thought he could play ball, but now a man who can really play ball commands a better salary than a college president. The times have changed, and today, anyone who hopes to succeed or even keep up with the procession must have a thorough knowledge of his calling.

Now, I contend that the church should not be behind the world. We, too, need trained workmen. From every quarter, the same complaint arises that churches are not able to find competent men for superintendents, Bible teachers, and leaders in Christian work. Good men are plenty, men of intelligence and consecration. They know something about the Bible, too, but they do not know how to use it or apply it to the conscience in a way to produce results. The Bible is often called the sword of the Spirit, but of what use is a sword to one who has not taken fencing lessons? His opponent can disarm him in a moment and leave him utterly defenseless. Even so, many Christians who might wield the sword of the Spirit with tremendous power are almost impotent for the lack of a little special training in using the Bible.

The Bible is often called the sword of the Spirit, but of what use is a sword to one who has not taken fencing lessons?

The day has gone by when the world is coming to the church for the gospel. The only alternative is for the church to carry the gospel to the world. But who is to do it? The ministers have about all they can do. If it is done at all, it is evident that the laity must be pressed more and more into the service. However, the work is too important to be entrusted to bungling hands. Shall men be trained for baseball and boating and not be trained to win souls? God forbid. Wherever else cheap labor may answer, it will not suffice here.

I am convinced that one reason more Christians do not engage in personal work is the consciousness of their unfitness for the work and the fear of failure in it. Indeed, I have heard ministers confess that they did not introduce the subject of religion because they feared they might not be able to answer the questions raised. The ignorance of the Bible, which prevails among intelligent people, would be amusing, if it were not so painful.

I was once summoned to talk with a dying man. He had suffered a severe hemorrhage, and it was thought he had only a short time to live. As I entered the room, he sat in a chair bolstered with pillows, and his face was almost as white as the pillows themselves. I said, "Poor fellow, you are having a hard time, aren't you?" I looked around for a Bible. His wife handed me one, saying, "I have just been reading to him from the Bible." "What did you read?" I asked. "The first chapter of Genesis." "Do you mean to say that you read the first chapter of Genesis to your husband?" "Yes," she said, "I thought I would begin at the beginning."

I was amazed for consider what the first chapter of Genesis says. *In the beginning God created the heavens and the earth. The earth was formless and void, and darkness was over the surface of the deep, and the Spirit of God was moving over the surface of the waters.* It is all the Word of God and of blessed inspiration, but think of giving that to an unsaved man for a dying pillow! Yet, that was his own wife doing the best she knew how, and she had attended church and Sunday School all her life. It did not take five minutes to lead the man to Christ, but I confess that I could not have done it with the first chapter of Genesis.

Professor Agassiz, when asked what his greatest work in this country was, replied, "The scientific training of three men. One of them abandoned my theories entirely, and another renounced my friendship. Nevertheless, I consider my greatest achievement in this country to be the scientific training of these three men." Is there not a lesson here for pastors? Is it not evident that they must do more teaching in the future, even if they do sacrifice some of the preaching? One trained worker is worth a dozen ordinary Christians, and there are scores of choice young men and women in our churches who would welcome instruction in the use of God's Word if it were offered to them.

I know of a training class from which three young men started for the ministry, two young women went into mission work, and one offered herself for the foreign field. Out of another class of sixteen members, two became ministers, twelve went to the foreign field, one became a trained nurse, and one is the religious reporter on a daily paper. Another class of twenty members sent nearly all of them into some form of Christian work. The fact is that when people know how to do Christian work well, they love to do it. Why not have a training class in your church? These are stirring times, and God needs every available worker. Will you be one and advocate for a training class in your community until you get it?

1. The object. The object of a training class is to teach Christians how to use the Bible in personal work. A man might own a whole drugstore, but he would be of little use to the sick if he did not know where to find the drugs or their various medicinal properties. Even so, a Christian may have a Bible that contains remedies for every conceivable spiritual condition, but if he does not know where to find them or how to use them, he will have little success as a soul winner. The training class shows how to diagnose a case, what remedies to use, and where to find them.

Furthermore, it awakens an interest in religious work, which nothing else will. It is a law of human nature that when one first learns how to do anything, he is eager to try it.

My experience shows that just as soon as a Christian knows how to lead another to Christ or deal with any spiritual difficulty, he goes about looking for a job. If all our church members were thus watching for souls, a great many more would be saved, and their own souls would be wonderfully enlarged.

2. The method. If an hour a week can be secured for the meeting, it would be well to spend the first part in the study of some book of the Bible, taking a few chapters each week, and carefully studying their contents. Some might prefer to take up the study of doctrine. The Moody Bible Institute has a number of courses in the study of the Bible and methods of Christian work. They have a course on personal work and one on evangelism, the latter prepared by the author of this volume. For information, address the Correspondence Department, 153 Institute Place, Chicago.

The latter part of the hour should be devoted to typical cases, such as those who are indifferent to religion, those who wish to be saved, but do not know how, those who have difficulties, the excuse-makers, those who are resting on false hopes, or those who hold erroneous views of the Bible. In the treatment of these cases, consider first the cause. What is the probable cause of this condition of mind? There may be many possible causes, and it is well to consider all that can be suggested. This affords a fine opportunity for the study of human nature and character analysis.

After discussing the possible causes, take up the cure. There must be a cure somewhere in the Bible. What is it, and where is it? Some will suggest one passage and some another. Compare them carefully, decide which is best, and put the result in your notebook. Ask the class what examples can be found in Scripture which illustrate the case in hand. Ask them if they know personally any case of this kind.

Select two or three verses for each character, and require the class to commit them to memory. Review them all at each meeting until every member can give them accurately with chapter and verse. Some may think it unnecessary to learn chapter and verse, but insist upon it, and soon they will recognize its value. If they write the verses for each week on a card and carry it with them, they can easily commit them at odd moments.

Occasionally, it is good for the leader to impersonate a character. He can say, "Now, class, tonight I will assume that I am an infidel or a spiritualist. You claim to be Christians. Convince me that I am wrong and lead me to your position." This is a fine practice for the class, and enables the leader to point out any flaw in their argument or any inaccuracy of statement. For instance, one might claim that the Bible was inspired, and the leader would reply, "I do not believe it. It may be that God could inspire a little pile of paper, but I doubt if He ever did." "Oh, I mean that the authors of the Bible were inspired." "Well, if that is what you mean, why not say so? Learn to be exact in your statements."

If one cannot get an evening for such a class, I see no reason a pastor could not take fifteen minutes out of the midweek meeting for this work. If necessary, the Scripture reading might be omitted for this work is all Scripture. Let the pastor show his people one night how to lead a soul to Christ, using the blackboard and putting on it two or three verses. The following week, he could call for the verses and make the whole company repeat them until all were familiar with them and then take up some of the excuses that arise in dealing with the unconverted. There would still be ample time for prayer and testimony, and at the close each one could be urged to put in practice what they had learned that night. I was suggesting this course in a ministers' meeting in Chicago, when one of them told me that he had been trying it a few weeks, and the attendance had increased threefold.

Chapter 24

Learning to Pray

The disciples one day overheard the Master's private devotions. So impressive was the scene that when He ceased, they came to Him, saying, "Lord, teach us to pray." Without a moment's hesitation apparently, He gave them, first, what we might call "The Model Prayer." Second, He gave them a striking illustration of the value of intercessory prayer. Third, He taught them concerning the chief object of prayer, which is the Holy Spirit. Indeed, this eleventh chapter of Luke contains the most comprehensive teachings on prayer in the Bible.

Where is the great Teacher now? Seated at the right hand of God, where *He always lives to make intercession for them* (Heb. 7:25). If our spiritual ears could be opened and we could hear Him as He pleads for us and the lost world, I am sure our hearts would grow tender and our eyes moist. With trembling lips, we, too, should say, "Lord, teach us how to pray."

We remember how Abraham prayed Lot out of Sodom, and Nehemiah prayed himself into the good graces of the king. Elijah shut up the heavens for three years, and the friends of Peter prayed him out of prison. All these were men of like passions with ourselves. Lord, teach us how to pray. Yes, to "pray." We can recall many utterances which pass for prayer but which we fear the Master would not recognize as such: selfish and thoughtless prayers that had no aim or purpose, prayers from which we did not expect an answer, did not look for an answer, and would have been mightily surprised if an answer had come.

All these have gone up to the mercy seat with our names upon them, and there they lie in the archives of heaven unanswered because they are unanswerable. Oh, friends, it is one thing to make a prayer; it is quite another thing to pray. Lord, teach us how to pray. How suggestive that phrase is, "Make a prayer," as if a prayer could be made to order, whether there was any occasion for it or not! But to pray, to really talk with God and bring things to pass, is a privilege that angels might covet and an art worthy of a lifetime of study.

To pray, to really talk with God and bring things to pass, is a privilege that angels might covet.

The Chinese write their prayers on bits of paper and throw them into the air, hoping they may be blown up to heaven. The Hindoos have praying machines and express their devotion by turning a crank. The followers of Mohammed fall upon their knees five times a day wherever they are at the hour of prayer and call upon God. Roman Catholics in Mexico take off their hats when the clock strikes twelve because it was at noon that our Savior was placed upon the Cross, and again when the clock strikes three because, at that hour, the Son of God died for our sins. Yes, there are prayers enough, but not enough praying. Lord, teach us how to pray.

How much we need to be taught! How often do we ask for

things that are better for us not to have, while the things we need most are seldom mentioned? Paul was right when he said, "We do not know how to pray as we should." How little do we realize the willingness of God to answer prayer! Too often, He is addressed as a capricious tyrant from whom blessings can be obtained only by persistent teasing instead of a loving Father who lives and labors for His children's welfare. How little we perceive the scope of the promises! We see the surface meaning, perhaps, but the depths – oh, the depths! How little we understand the deep things of God!

How little do we understand the relation of prayer to Christian work. The common idea is that work is the main business of a Christian, and a little prayer is necessary to help the work along. Work is the strong bow that supplies the force to speed the arrow on its way, while prayer is the feather that tips the arrow and helps guide it to its destined mark. Christ's idea is entirely different. In His conception, prayer is the chief business of a Christian, with just enough work to make a channel through which the spiritual forces generated by prayer may find an outlet. Prayer is the bow that supplies the force, and work is the feather that guides the arrow towards its destination. *If you ask Me, I will do it* (John 14:14), He says. In other words, Christ is still doing the work that He *began to do* (Acts 1:1), and He invites us to help Him by prayer, whereas too many Christians think that they are carrying on the work but need a little help from Him. Your idea may best be determined by estimating the amount of time you spend working for the Lord and the amount of time spent in prayer.

Yes, we are ignorant, but thank God we can all learn. Jesus has opened a school of prayer in which, if we will, we may learn the divine art. And what a Teacher! How patient, how longsuffering with dull scholars! And how much He knows about the subject! For eighteen hundred years, this has been His constant occupation, and now He invites us to become His pupils and offers to teach us all He knows. *All things that I have heard from My Father I have made known unto you* (John 15:15).

What a privilege! We need not leave home either to enter this school. We need to use no expense save that of time, but we must take time. Take time to be holy, for a holy life is the only soil where faith grows. Take time to study the promises, for their meaning lies hidden from the careless reader. Take time to commune with God, for to know Him and be well acquainted with Him are the great secrets of success. Let us all join the Master's School of Prayer and take a series of lessons. Surely, we all need it, and there is room for all, not in a seat but a kneeling place, for in this school we study upon our knees, with the Bible as a textbook.

> "O Thou by whom we come to God –
> The Life, the Truth, the Way –
> The path of prayer Thyself hast trod;
> Lord, teach us how to pray."

Chapter 25

The Element of Time in Prayer

S ome requests are answered very quickly. A lady was once giving an address on narcotics. At the close, a young man said to her, "I do not think it is wrong for me to use tobacco."

"Are you a Christian?" she asked.

"Yes," was the reply.

"Have you ever asked God for His opinion?"

"No."

"Well, if you are a Christian, I suppose you are willing to leave the matter to His decision. Let us kneel right down here and ask Him. I will pray first, and then you can follow."

The young man could not consistently refuse. He knelt with her, and at the close of her prayer, he began to pray. He had not uttered three sentences before he sprang to his feet, saying, "I see it. It is not right. I will give it up at once."

In this case, prayer was answered immediately, but in many cases, the answer is long delayed.

As I left a meeting a few weeks ago, where plans had been matured for opening a mission, a lady whose sister had consented to take charge of the work said to me, "This is the answer to seven years of prayer. All this time, I have been asking God to lead my sister into this work, and now she is as anxious to enter upon it as I was to have her." Had she ceased praying before the seven years expired, who can say what the result would have been?

When Mr. George Muller was in this country, a friend of mine asked him how long he had ever prayed continuously for any object. Taking a little book from his pocket, he said, "When I was converted, I was a wild boy in college. My conversion broke a friendship between my roommate and myself, for he 'would have nothing to do with such a fanatic,' he said. I wrote his name in this book and promised God that I would pray for him each day until he was converted or I died. I prayed five years with no apparent result. Ten years went by with no change. I continued on for fifteen years, then twenty years, and still he was an unbeliever. I did not yet give him up but prayed twenty-five years, each day mentioning his name at the throne of grace. Then came a letter saying, 'I have found the Savior.' Then," said Mr. Muller, "I checked out this petition as answered. In this same book, I have other names that I have prayed for five, ten, and fifteen years, and scores of names against which there is a cross, showing that the requests have been granted."

Here then was a man who made a business of prayer and kept his accounts with the Lord in a businesslike way. When he had a matter to present to God's attention, he first found a promise on which to base his appeal, always making sure, if possible, that it was according to God's will. Then he recorded his petition in a book and watched and waited for the answer.

Is it any wonder that this man's faith grew rapidly and that he became the most notable and possibly the most successful pray-er of modern times?

We see by this illustration why many prayers fail. They are rambling appeals, so vague and indefinite that even the petitioner can hardly remember what he prayed for when he rises from his knees. No record is made of them since we do not expect an answer, and no surprise is felt if the answer does not come. And so the solemn farce goes on year after year.

It is said that in battle, it takes a hundred pounds of lead to kill a man because ninety-nine pounds and fifteen ounces of it is wasted in wild firing that aims at nothing and hits no one. On the other hand, the sharpshooter wastes no ammunition but picks his man and makes every bullet tell. So, if we would pray for fewer objects, more carefully selected, and then make a record of our prayers and watch for the answer, we should not waste our breath and would obtain more results.

Delays in answered prayer often prove to be a great blessing to us. In some cases, it tests the strength of our desire. It shows us that we did not care very much about the object after all, just *In some cases, delays in* as a request for an education that is *answered prayer tests the* soon dropped shows the parent that *strength of our desire.* the boy was not earnest enough to appreciate the privilege if he had it. In other cases, delay leads us to examine our motives, and we find that they are purely or partially selfish and withdraw the request of our own accord. Possibly, the delay opens our eyes to some secret sin and leads us to abandon it, for *If I regard wickedness in my heart, The Lord will not hear* (Psalm 66:18).

Sometimes, we find that our heart is not fully consecrated, and we are led to take an advanced step. And in every case, delayed answers keep us waiting long at the feet of Jesus and compel us to become better acquainted with Him. Unconsciously, we learn something of His patience, faith, and humility. Someone has said that prayers which are soon answered are like coastal vessels that soon return laden with coal and lumber, while others, like ships from Africa or India, are longer on the way, but bring back a richer cargo of gold and gems.

Then, too, we should remember that God often answers prayers through natural laws, which work slowly. God does not force a man's will but wooes him by love and persuasion. Man is a creature of growth, and it takes time, change, children, and often losses, bereavements, and old age to soften his heart and show him his need of a Savior. Consider how many influences wrought upon you before you yielded, how many appeals were made, how many times the still small voice whispered before you answered "Yes." Considering all this, you will not wonder that it takes time for God to answer prayer which involves the change of a human will from disobedience to obedience. Give him time and do not, like foolish children, be anxious to pick the apple before it is ripe.

If you ask why our will should count for anything with God, remember first, that we come in the name of His Son, and second, that He has promised that *the prayer of a righteous man can accomplish much*, and third, that when we have but one desire, namely to know and do His will, God's will has really become our will. Then it is eminently safe and reasonable for Him to say, *ask whatever you wish, and it will be done for you* (John 15:7). When the child of God is so zealous for God's will as to care more for it than for his own, then God promotes him to share in the administration of the affairs of this world and to become an open channel for the communication of His grace.

Lord, teach us how to pray.

Chapter 26

The Master's Reception Evening

1. The ideal prayer meeting never happens. If it is a good meeting, somebody has put prayer, thought, and work into it. The laws of grace are as rigid and reliable as the laws of nature. "Heaven may be had for asking," says the poet, but the ideal prayer meeting cannot. It is as true here as elsewhere that *"whatever a man sows, that he will also reap* (Gal. 6:7).

Hence, the leader should prepare carefully. The hymns can be selected; one person can be asked to pray for the sick, another for the absent, and so on. Attention to detail helps immensely. The leader should wait upon God in prayer until his heart burns with love and his soul is sensitive to the faintest whisper of the Holy Spirit. If athletes train for a boat race or a ball game simply to secure the applause of people, surely the Christian can afford to train for a spiritual conflict where all the forces of heaven and hell are arrayed against each other, where eternal destinies are at stake, and where every part of the service is watched with keenest solicitude by *so great a cloud of witnesses*.

Not only the leader but also the members should prepare. Let them read, think, and pray over the subject. Let them deny themselves daily, for a godly life is the best preparation for an ideal meeting. Let them gather up spiritual strength through the week and concentrate it upon this service, making it the supreme hour of the week, the hour

"When heaven comes down our souls to greet,
And glory crowns the mercy seat."

2. The ideal prayer meeting has an object as well as a subject, a definite object never to be forgotten by the leader or the workers.

What is that object? It is not simply to have an interesting meeting. A service may be interesting and yet be so devoid of spirituality as to suggest only *a noisy gong or a clanging cymbal*. The real object is to awaken spiritual emotion, bring the soul face to face with God, and kindle the fires of devotion until the altar is all ablaze with the sacrifice of willing hearts. There comes over the audience that indescribable thrill and holy hush that reveals the presence of God and which makes every heart ready to say, "O God, Thy will be done."

The real object of a prayer meeting is to bring the soul face to face with God.

This is the true object of a prayer meeting – to bring every soul to the point where it is willing to do its duty so that decisions may be made and results may be secured right then and there. At the close of a meeting where the theme was temperance, the tide of feeling rose so high that sixty-four young men and women signed a total abstinence pledge and thereby completely revolutionized the temperance sentiment of that church.

Whatever the subject of the meeting, never lose sight of the object. Feeling which does not lead to action is of questionable value.

3. The ideal meeting is cheerful, social, and hearty. Have a nice carpet on the floor, appropriate pictures on the wall, flowers on the table, and the room seated with chairs. Make it look as little like a church and as much like a home as possible. Take off your hats, coats, and overshoes. Let the whole atmosphere of the service be bright, breezy, and cheerful.

Have a "smile-'em-up committee" at the door to welcome strangers and to distribute the audience wisely: the small boys apart from each other, the workers near the unconverted, and the timid ones near the more spiritual. The man at the door needs to have the skill of a general and a face as bright as the headlight of an engine.

Into this "rest for the weary" come with your thanksgiving and rejoicing. Make the heavens ring with song. Let the most spiritual members lead in prayer until a strong devotional atmosphere has been created, making it easy for anyone to confess Christ.

Be simple and, above all, sincere, especially in prayer. Remember the Quaker who was to share a room with another at a convention. After they had knelt and prayed, the Quaker took his hat and prepared to depart. "Hold on," said the other, "I thought you were going to spend the night with me." "I was," said the Quaker, "but since I heard you pray, I have changed my mind. If you are the kind of man you said you were in your prayer, I am afraid to sleep with you."

Be cheerful! Paul had his discouragements, but he kept them to himself. Cultivate the habit of hand shaking and do not wait for an introduction. In short, strive to be

> "One of the spirits chosen by heaven to turn
> The sunny side of things to human eyes."

4. The ideal meeting is one in which everyone takes part. There are some things that lie within everyone's reach. You can fill up the front seats and thus support the leader. You can speak early in the meeting, for one sentence then is worth a dozen later.

Anyone can repeat a verse of Scripture, and if it is selected with care and prayer, God will use it to strengthen the saints and to carry conviction to sinners. Remember that the Word of God is the sword of the Spirit. Use it for a purpose, and expect results.

No believer should be satisfied until he is able to express the feelings which the Spirit awakens in his heart. Expression is the law of spiritual growth. The Dead Sea is dead because it has no outlet, and even the Water of Life will grow stagnant unless it is shared with other hearts. Therefore, *Let the redeemed of the Lord say so* (Psalm 107:2). Jesus Christ is on trial before the world, and we are His witnesses. If we know anything in His favor, let us speak it out, remembering always that one word of testimony is worth an hour of talk.

Expression is the law of spiritual growth.

Finally, I believe that everyone can, if he will, learn to pray in public. In a Christian Endeavour Society numbering eighty active members, everyone learned to lead in public worship. Some formed a little prayer circle for private practice. At first, a few wrote out their thoughts and read them. Others resorted to the Prayer Book, while others took a verse of Scripture and converted it into a prayer, until at length, like Paul's sailors, some on boards and some on broken pieces of the ship, they all came safe to land.

Doubtless, it is hard for many, but why do we enlist if it is not to endure hardness? Mr. Edison tells us that in perfecting the phonograph he had great difficulty in making it produce the letter "s." "I said to it, 'specia, specia,' and the obstinate thing responded, 'pecia, pecia.' It was enough to try the patience of a saint, but I kept at it from eighteen to twenty hours a day for seven long months, and at length, I conquered it." If one can toil like that to overcome a mechanical difficulty, surely a Christian can afford to labor long to fit himself for the Master's service.

When Mary was looking for a present for the Lord, she did not buy the cheapest box of perfume. She kept inquiring if there was anything better until the merchant brought out the alabaster box, saying, we can imagine, "This is the finest thing in the market, but it is very expensive. The price is three hundred pence." "Never mind," said Mary. "It is none too good for Jesus." So she took it home and broke it at the Master's feet, and the perfume of it is spreading still, though losing nothing of its sweetness.

At a meeting held one hot night in August, the leader read this story and suggested that each one break an alabaster box by offering that service that would cost him the most. Prayer after prayer was poured into the ear of One who was felt to be present. It seemed like the Day of Pentecost. When the roll was examined, it was found that of the fifty-three active members present, forty-four had offered prayer, seven had given testimonies, and two quotations of prose or poetry. It was an ideal prayer meeting. When we come to the Master's "Reception evening," may you and I, dear friend, break an "alabaster box" at His feet.

Chapter 27

Leaflet Evangelism

The indiscriminate use of tracts by those whose zeal exceeds their wisdom has led many good people to question their value. It is foolish, however, to allow our prejudice against poor tracts to blind us to the value of good ones, and good ones can be had. The choicest thoughts of the best writers can now be found in leaflet form, and many a soul has been awakened by one of these silent messengers that God has put into the hand at just the right moment.

A man stepped into a street car in New York and, before taking his seat, gave each passenger a little card bearing the words, "Look to Jesus when tempted, when troubled, when dying." One of the passengers carefully read the card and put it in his pocket. As he left the car, he said to the giver, "Sir, when you gave me this card, I was on my way to the ferry, intending to jump from the boat and drown myself. The death of my wife and son had robbed me of all desire to live, but this card has persuaded me to begin life anew. Good day, and God bless you."

There is no such thing as chance in this world, and those who seek to be led by the Spirit often find themselves messengers of mercy to some weary soul. A lady once traveled two hundred miles to tell the writer personally how a card he had given her had led to her conversion. It lay in her bureau drawer, bearing its silent testimony from time to time as she read it until it finally led her to Christ.

Those who seek to be led by the Spirit often find themselves messengers of mercy to some weary soul.

Some ministers make constant use of leaflets in their pastoral work. They open the way for conversation and are often better than words, for a soul under conviction is sometimes disposed to quarrel, but one cannot quarrel with a tract. It never loses its temper, never answers back, and sticks to what it has said. Besides, you can send a leaflet to many places where you cannot go yourself.

People in sorrow or sickness love to be remembered, and boys think more of a minister who occasionally gives them a bright leaflet. A man wrote me that in a town where he had used "Why a Boy Should Be a Christian," forty-five people, on their examination for church membership, testified that they attributed their conversion mainly to that leaflet.

Housekeepers can use tracts to good advantage. Lay them on the parlor table so that callers may read them while waiting. Often, there is enough time for one to be converted while a lady is preparing for her visitors. Give them to the milkman, the grocer, and the postman; enclose them in letters, library books, and packages.

Businessmen have fine opportunities for this kind of work. A man once said, "I cannot speak in meetings, but if you will supply me with choice reading matter, I will pay for it and enclose it in the packages which go out of my store." Recently, a customer uttered an oath in a New York business house. The proprietor quietly handed him a tract entitled "Why Do You Swear?" The man read it, tears came to his eyes, and he said, "I beg your pardon, sir." "Never mind me," said the other, "but don't you think you had better ask for God's pardon? It was His name that you profaned." "I will do it, sir," said the man, and he shook his hand warmly. It is not easy to rebuke a swearer, but anyone can say, "Here is a leaflet which you may find helpful," or he can mail one to every profane person he knows.

Teachers can make good use of leaflets. Those who cannot talk with their pupils can put into their hands the wise words of others. Old-fashioned tracts will not do for boys. They want something that sparkles with life, rivets attention, and stops when it gets there.

We all know this is a busy age. People have no time, or think that they do not, to read books on religion, but if you put into their hands something attractive, interesting, and which can be read in a few minutes, it is sure of attention. I am convinced that anyone can easily multiply his influence twentyfold by a wise use of printer's ink.

J. Hudson Taylor, the founder of the great China Inland Mission, was converted by a leaflet when he was fifteen years old. Dr. R. A. Torrey, dean of the Bible Institute of Los Angeles, says that there are two kinds of ammunition that he always carries with him: the Bible and a package of leaflets.

A ticket agent who gave away a tract with every ticket sold said that over twenty persons wrote him saying the leaflets he gave them had been blessed to their conversion.

One of the greatest secrets of success in Christian work is to have something to give away. Thus, you can always secure attention, even among strangers, and open the way for conversation. With a kindly smile, you can hand one a leaflet, saying, "Would you like something to read?" After it is read, the most natural thing is to talk about it. By offering a tract, I have often detained people at the close of a service and thus found an opportunity for Christian conversation. In this way, nine people recently remained to get a leaflet, and all of them knelt with me and accepted Christ.

Never give away a tract unless you know its contents. Use all the tact you have and pray for more. An old man said to a train boy, "No, I don't want your popcorn. Don't you see I haven't any teeth?" "Buy some gum drops then, nice fresh gum drops." That boy knew how to adapt himself to his customers, and so should we. Occasionally, select a good tract and print the name of your church or Sunday School on it with an invitation to attend the services, canvass the whole neighborhood, and leave a tract at every house.

A physician told me recently that three times in three different cities, and at intervals of about a year, someone put into his pocket without his knowledge a little blue card containing the words, "Have you a home in heaven, where the angels are, and where your mother is, etc.?" The first two cards made him think, but the third came when he had just lost his mother, and it led him to Christ. None of the three people knew that they were supplementing each other's work, yet they were. None of the three ever knew that any good came from the card that they dropped into the stranger's pocket, but he knew, God knew, and that was enough. We shall never know all the good that comes from this kind of silent preaching, but we know enough to make it almost criminal for us to neglect it.

Chapter 28

Letter Writing as a Means of Winning Souls

Few people realize how much Christian work can be accomplished by letter writing. In some cases, a letter is better than words, for it can be read, re-read, and pondered at one's leisure. Henry Clay Trumbull says he was led to Christ by a personal appeal in a letter from a friend. What preaching and the ordinary forms of church work had not accomplished for him was done by a few sentences in a note. As he reflected upon this, he began to realize the importance of individual work for individuals, and he engaged in this form of effort all his life.

A prominent businessman in Worcester, Mass., went to his pastor and said that he would like to unite with the church. When asked how long he had been a Christian, he replied that he had taken the step only a few days ago and was led to do this at the request of a lady who had written him on the subject.

He said that sermons had not made much impression on him, but this letter from a person whom he hardly knew appealed to him so strongly that he could not resist it.

A little mission Sunday School in Connecticut organized a home department. One of the workers wrote to a friend who was living in the forests of Canada, far from any church, and asked if she would not like to join their home department. The reply was favorable, and the literature was sent. Soon, the friend in Canada wrote that she thought she could get some of her neighbors to join the Connecticut school if she had the proper literature. In a short time, she succeeded in getting twenty-five more members, all of whom became identified with the little mission school in Connecticut, three or four hundred miles away.

They were so pleased with their work that after a while, they organized a Sunday School of their own. Soon, they outgrew their accommodations, raised money, and built a chapel. Then they said, "We ought to have a Christian Endeavour Society," and soon that, too, was organized. This went on for a while, but the more they studied the Bible, the more hungry they grew, and they eventually organized a church and secured a pastor. All this came from one letter written by an enterprising worker in a little school several hundred miles away.

If the subject were uppermost in one's mind, opportunities would frequently be found to say a word for Christ.

Why should Christians not aim to make their correspondence count for the Master as well as their conversation? There might be some letters in which it would not be advisable to introduce the subject of religion. However, on the other hand, if the subject were uppermost in one's mind, opportunities would frequently be found to say a word for Christ, drop a hint, or enclose a leaflet. I know a businessman who was writing a letter one day when he saw a tract on his table. He enclosed it and mailed the letter without much thought. Then the devil whispered to him, "You have made a fool of yourself. What do you suppose that man will think of you for putting a tract in a business letter?" Being a Christian, he lifted his heart in prayer to God, saying, "Lord, did I make a mistake?"

Back came the answer, "What is to hinder you from putting a tract in every letter you write?"

"By the grace of God, I will," he replied, and for the remainder of his life, he followed this practice. He saw so much good coming from this kind of effort that finally he withdrew from business and devoted his life to writing letters and sending out Christian literature of various kinds. Not everyone can do as this man did, but all can do something if they make the effort and pray for tact and guidance.

I know a lady who, to help a drinking man, took him into her family as a boarder. Soon, he committed some misdemeanor and was sent to prison. She did not forsake him in his disgrace, but remembering the Master's words, *I was sick, and you visited Me; I was in prison, and you came to Me* (Matt. 25:36), she endeavored to help him by writing encouraging letters. Soon, other prisoners requested that she write to them, and this work increased until she was writing between two and three hundred letters a year to the inmates of different prisons. Her aim was always to lead her correspondents to Christ, but her letters contained much kindly advice, and often, she sent little delicacies or reading matter that would interest them.

As soon as a prisoner was led to accept Christ, she sent him a Bible and concordance and tried to interest him in Bible study. If they showed much proficiency in this work, she entered their name in a Bible correspondence school that took her proteges at half price. Many of her correspondents became Bible teachers, and some had large classes in their respective prisons. Some of these prisoners, when their term of service expired, devoted their lives to Christian work, after taking a course of study in some institution. I have heard her say that there were eight pastors of churches who were converted while in state prison through her correspondence. Murderers, infidels, and hardened men of all kinds have been led to Christ by this humble woman through her prayers and letters.

She is a farmer's wife, has had only an ordinary education, and has taken in sewing and washing in order to earn money to pay the postage. I have even heard her say that there had been months when she could not write a single letter because she did not have the money to buy a postage stamp.

If God can so signally bless the work of this patient and humble worker, who is willing to make such sacrifices in order to help the unfortunate and criminal classes, should not others who have more time and money ask themselves what they can do to honor God in their correspondence?

Chapter 29

Open Air Work

With the coming of summer, church audiences begin to dwindle, and streets and parks begin to swarm with people. Nature spreads her carpet of green, and the air is soft and balmy. The birds sing, the flowers bloom, and everything seems to say, "Come out and enjoy life with us." Why should we try to resist this pleading and insist on holding all our religious services indoors simply because we always have done it?

Many a church would double its audience by holding an occasional service out of doors, under the trees, or in some adjacent park. If chairs can be provided, so much the better. If not, let the people sit on the grass as they did when Jesus preached. If the church has no convenient place for outdoor meetings, hold an open-air service on the porch before the evening meeting. Have plenty of good singing with two or three-minute addresses sandwiched between. In a little while, the children will gather, the passers will stop, the carriages will drive up, and you will have a large company of people, many of whom would never think of entering a church. If you have never tried it, begin this season.

Every church ought to have a band of open-air workers to hold meetings regularly all summer at such points as may seem most strategic. Some churches gain from fifty to a hundred new members each year by their open-air work. Even if they did not add a single convert, they would be well repaid for the effort in the benefit obtained by the workers. Then, too, it affords an outlet for the zeal, faith, and energy of the church. It puts new life into every department of work. The church begins to respect itself, for it is now working as aggressively as it should and is no longer content simply to hold its own. The outside world will soon recognize the difference and esteem it more highly.

Open-air workers should be carefully trained, for no work requires more tact, wisdom, and holy boldness.

Open-air workers should be carefully trained, for no work requires more tact, wisdom, and holy boldness. All kinds of talent can be used, which is another advantage. Those who cannot speak can sing, pray silently, give out Gospel cards, do personal work, or keep the children quiet. The following suggestions are taken from a book written by a very dear friend of mine, Henry B. Gibbud, called "Under the Blue Canopy of Heaven".

1. "Permit. In towns and cities, it is necessary to obtain a permit for street services. Have some one of influence apply for the permit. A politician is better for this work than a preacher.

2. "Place of Meeting. Go where the people are. It may be a noisy place, but you have the people. If you want quiet, go to the cemetery.

3. "Select a place where you have a building at your back. It will act as a sounding board for the voice. If possible, arrange the meeting so that you may also have a building in front of you. It is very hard to speak in the open air, and a building in front of you to throw the voice back will make it much easier.

4. "Talk with the wind always, and never against it.

5. "Select a place where the audience will be comfortable. Give them the shade even if you have to stand in the sun.

6. "Have bright, new, catchy songs. The audience, as a rule, does not join in the singing, so there is less need for familiar hymns.

7. "Speakers. Let them stand on a chair, box, or platform. Then your voice sounds out and over the crowd. All can see you, and you can see them. If any disturbance occurs, such as a dog fight, always give out a hymn. The song will put a new thought into the dog's mind and often break up the fight.

8. "Never ask questions of the crowd; you will get more than you bargained for. Do not stop to answer questions from the crowd, but courteously say that you will be glad to talk with the questioner after the service.

9. "Preach the Word. This old world is hungry for the plain gospel made fresh and vivid by actual experience. Use plenty of illustrations, but see that you have something to illustrate. Nothing grips an audience or holds attention like the simple gospel story told out of a warm heart.

10. "We do not open the meeting with prayer. Have much prayer before the meeting, and urge all workers who are not speaking to continue in silent prayer.

11. "Call for decisions at the close of the service, or invite into a church if another service is to follow. Let each worker select someone for personal effort when the meeting closes."

By offering to give away gospel cards or tracts at the close of the service, you can often hold the entire crowd to the very end. Show them the cards and read some of the titles, such as: "The Workingman's Trust. Are you in it?" "How Many Times Have you Been Born?" "The Three Cheers of Jesus," "Four Things Which One Ought to Know," "The Unanswerable Question," "Coffin Nails," "Morbus Sabbaticus, or Sunday Sickness," "Get Right With God," "God Wants the Boys," or "Only Three Steps into the Christian Life."

Chapter 30

Revivals and How to Secure Them

The word "revival" is associated in many minds with unpleasant recollections. It suggests a season of great excitement, the multiplication of meetings, a multitude hurried into the church, many of whom are not converted, followed by a reaction equally strong, and of much longer duration. Such a season all sensible people deprecate, but it is foolish to condemn all revivals because some are spurious. It would not be wise to refuse all money because we have seen a few counterfeit bills, but it would be wiser to learn the difference between genuine and counterfeit. Even so, it may be profitable to consider what a genuine revival of religion is, why it is often necessary, and what can be done to promote it.

A revival is simply a renewal of spiritual life that has grown dormant. Strictly speaking, it applies only to Christians because those with no spiritual life cannot have it renewed. You can revive a drooping plant but not a dead one. So those in whose heart Christ dwells may have their love for Him increased, but one who has never been converted cannot be revived. However, when Christians are revived, the unsaved are sure to be converted, though this is, by no means, the principal benefit.

That the Spirit does move upon a church or community at times in an unusual manner cannot be denied. In place of apathy and indifference, we see attention and interest. God's Word seems attractive, and God's house is thronged night after night regardless of the weather or the season. Old feuds are forgotten, old enemies are reconciled, and everybody feels that they ought to settle up with God and man, whether it involves a hearty confession, the paying of a debt, or the restoration of that which has been wrongfully taken. The atmosphere is favorable to the confession of Christ, and those who have long felt it to be their duty are now emboldened to do it. If all this makes better men and women, more considerate parents, more obedient children, happier homes, and more peaceful neighborhoods, who shall say that it is not an unmixed blessing? Anything that makes people more reverent and prayerful or more honest and truthful is good and good only. This is precisely what a revival of religion does.

Objection 1. It awakens excitement. What if it does? Excitement is a good thing if the object is a worthy one, and the conversion of lost men and women is certainly a worthy object. Businessmen try constantly to interest people in their stock of goods and work night and day to get a crowd into their store. Politicians flood the country with literature and parade the street with bands, and no one questions the wisdom of it because we know it is necessary to arouse the public to the importance of voting aright. However, when God's people put forth special efforts to arrest the attention of the thoughtless, the cry of excitement is sure to be raised. It is the devil's device to hinder the Lord's work, and he often finds professing Christians his best helpers in raising this foolish objection.

Objection 2. It does not last long. That may be true in some cases, but the merchant does not stop advertising his business because he knows the boom will not last long, nor does the politician, though he knows the campaign will be short. It is not to be expected that special meetings will continue for many weeks, but if the work is genuine, the results will abide for years. The Reformation lasted only a few years, but Europe and the whole world feel its effects to this hour. Pentecost lasted but a day, but in that day it changed the whole face of the world religiously.

If the work is genuine, the results will abide for years.

Why Are Revivals Necessary?

Why does a dying plant need water and sunshine? Because it does not have enough strength to hold its head up and must have outside help. Likewise, there are many Christians who are not self-sustaining. They do not pray or feed on the Word enough to keep them in good spiritual condition. The consequence is that they steadily lose ground until they are in danger of losing all hold on Christ, and special measures must be used to revive them. Frequent doses of God's Word must be poured into them until they begin to respond to it, love it, and become self-sustaining Christians, able to help others into the way of life.

In all ages, God has found it necessary to say to His church, *Awake, awake, Clothe yourself in your strength, O Zion; Clothe yourself in your beautiful garments, O Jerusalem, the holy city* (Isaiah 52:1).

When May a Revival Be Expected?

When God's people desire a revival and are willing to comply with the conditions. God is always willing, but His people are not. If *My people who are called by My name humble themselves and pray and seek My face and turn from their wicked ways, then I will hear from heaven, will forgive their sin and will heal their land* (2 Chron. 7:14).

> *"Bring the whole tithe into the storehouse, so that there may be food in My house, and test Me now in this," says the* LORD *of hosts, "if I will not open for you the windows of heaven and pour out for you a blessing until it overflows"* (Mal. 3:10).

These two passages seem to teach clearly that God's people can have a revival whenever they are willing to do their duty as the Word requires and claim God's promise. Oh, for a revival in every heart, home, and church in our land!

Do You Really Want a Revival?

A revival is not a thing of chance. If it comes, it is because someone has set in motion spiritual forces which make a revival inevitable.

On one occasion, when Dr. Lyman Beecher was pastor at Litchfield, Conn., a remarkable work of grace occurred. Its coming was sudden and unexpected. There had been no extra meetings, nor were there any indications of special interest such as usually precede an outpouring of the Spirit. No one could account for this strange manifestation of divine power.

When the interest had somewhat subsided, Dr. Beecher began to take up his pastoral work again and called, among other places, at the house of a sick man who lived on the outskirts of the parish. The shut-in asked many questions about the revival and the various people who had been converted and then told his pastor the following story.

He said that as he lay on his bed, he had felt greatly depressed at the thought of his utter uselessness. Finally, it occurred to him that he could at least pray for people if he could not visit and talk with them. He began to pray for his next-door neighbor, then the next house, and the next, until he had prayed his way to the end of the street, taking in every family and praying for every individual so far as he knew them. Then he took another street and another until he prayed his way all through the parish. Then he began again and prayed his way through the parish a second time. Then came the revival which he was expecting but which the church and pastor had no intimation of and for which, indeed, they do not appear to have been responsible.

When Dr. Beecher heard that story, he said: "Now I know where that revival had its earthly origin. It was in the sick room of that godly man."

Our Savior has an intense concern for souls. During His earthly life, He worked so zealously that He reminded His disciples of the passage, *Zeal for Your house will consume me* (John 2:17). He arose early in the morning to pray; indeed, he often prayed all night, we may believe. He wept over Jerusalem. He even sweat blood under the crushing weight of His personal responsibility.

Christ expects His church to share this concern for souls with Him.

Christ expects His church to share this concern for souls with Him. The church is the bride of Christ and the mother of God's children. A husband and wife ought to think alike and feel alike. Their interests are identical, and their hearts should throb as one. Unless the bride of Christ shares with her Lord in this concern for souls, no spiritual children will be born, for children are not born of one parent in either the natural or the spiritual world. Indeed, it would be a calamity if children should be born under such conditions. You might as well put a babe in the arms of a dead mother as to put converts into the care of a cold, unsympathizing church.

Those with experience know that the hardest thing to accomplish in revival work is to secure a favorable atmosphere for the new birth. After that, the work is very easy.

On the other hand, where there is a real concern for souls, conversions will occur.

A wife in England resolved to pray for her husband's conversion every day for a year. At the end of that period, he was apparently as far from Christ as ever. She decided that she would try it six months longer. At the end of that time, her husband was still indifferent. She was discouraged and thought she might as well give up. However, when she faced the question of giving up as lost the one whom God had manifestly entrusted to her spiritual care, she said to herself, "No, I will never give him up. I will pray for him as long as I live."

That very day, when her husband came home to dinner, he passed her in the hall and went upstairs. She waited for him until she became alarmed and then went up to his room. There was her husband on his knees, crying to God for mercy. He became an earnest Christian worker.

As soon as Zion travailed, she also brought forth her sons (Isaiah 66:8). Let us not look for the twentieth-century revival until we have become revived ourselves, for conviction of sin will not come to others until a concern for souls has come to us.